"Greg Winkler's Transformational Coach gives a full spectrum outlook on what coaching entails. Winkler takes the reader on a path through his experiences, challenges, and discoveries in the coaching world. He creates a holistic coaching model focused on progressive behaviors that speaks to today's athlete. This is a must read for coaches as it offers up solutions to modern challenges in the coaching world of today."

–Mike Juels, President and CEO, GAMEBREAKER

"Helping coaches master the qualities that inspire players and deliver the joy youngsters deserve from sports is a far more challenging task than teaching Xs and Os. Greg Winkler succeeds. After reading Greg Winkler, the complexities of coaching for success while delivering the enjoyable and nurturing environment that children deserve no longer seems so daunting."

–Mike Wiollta, Executive Editor, Soccer America Magazine

"I read this book from the 'new' coach perspective where we tend to worry more about the 'how to' of everything rather than the 'who am I coaching?' This book addresses the how and the who, the powerful and pertinent questions we should be asking as we seek transformation in ourselves and subsequently our impact on the players and community. This is the type of book that I know beyond a doubt will transform the way coaches at it any level can find mindfulness in what they do every day. If you coach, manage, or lead others, you will benefit greatly from this work."

–Miguel Dotres, CIC, Charlotte County Soccer Federation,
Vice President of Recreational Soccer – South

I0808522

This book is dedicated to my family who were instrumental in my coaching journey, a journey that still continues today, most especially to my wife, Vikki, who knows firsthand what it means to be a coaching widow.

As I reach a new stage in my life – grandparenthood – I also dedicate this book to Sophia, Rocco, and Oliver, and any future little ones. It is my hope that the coaches, teachers, and role models they have in their lives lead them with a transformational heart.

GREG WINKLER

The Transformational COACH

Incorporating Mindfulness for Improved Performance

MEYER & MEYER SPORT

British Library Cataloguing in Publication Data

A catalogue record for this book is available from the British Library

The Transformational Coach

Maidenhead: Meyer & Meyer Sport (UK) Ltd., 2021

ISBN: 978-1-78255-205-5

Aachen, Auckland, Beirut, Cairo, Cape Town, Dubai, Hägendorf, Hong Kong, Indianapolis, Maidenhead, Manila, New Delhi, Singapore, Sydney, Tehran, Vienna

Member of the World Sports Publishers' Association (WSPA), www.w-s-p-a.org

Printed by Books International

ISBN: 978-1-78255-205-5

Email: info@m-m-sports.com

www.thesportspublisher.com

CONTENTS

ACKNOWLEDGEMENTS

Special thanks to Nicole Dotres for taking my "brain" idea and creating a visual that represents the many areas a leader has to recognize to be truly mindful. Also to her husband Miguel Dotres for being the first to do a read through to help me examine the areas a new coach has to be aware of. Miguel is also the one who holds me accountable while I pace on the sidelines.

Thanks to two colleagues, Teresa Palmer and Mike Mitchell. Mike helped brainstorm the key areas that would be put into "the Brain." Teresa did a read-through to make sure I was on point with my mindfulness message.

Two of my family members: my wife Vikki who is my ultimate proof-reader and life partner. She has lived this journey. She has been through all of the highs and lows a coaching life has to offer. My son Brett who, despite his busy schedule, provided feedback and editorial advice throughout the process.

INTRODUCTION

"Coaches have a responsibility to create an environment where players are free to be creative and make in-moment game decisions."

Welcome to the Transformational Journey

You are about to take a literary journey to improve on your influence over the people that you lead. This book is a leadership guide; whether you are a coach of youth, high school-age, college-age, or professional athletes, there is a pathway to excellence and influence. You may not coach in the athletic arena, but as a teacher, an administrator, or a business leader, the lessons from athletic pursuits have always correlated with the classroom or the boardroom. You will find the following definitions helpful as we attempt to dig deeper and embark on this path to transformational leadership.

Transformational Coaching

A style of leadership in which the leader identifies the needed change, creates a vision to guide the change through inspiration, and executes the move with the commitment of the members of the group. (Business Directory Definition)

When a coach reaches this level of leadership, they have realized that coaching was never about them. Coaching/leadership was never intended to be about the leader's ego; it was always supposed to be a path to developing individuals through sport. My father wanted me to participate in athletics because sports were supposed to build character. My father grew up in the late 40s and 50s. His coaches demanded respect and responsibility; most of the coaches in that period did so with command-style leadership. It was a post-World War II era with an emerging Korean War. Young men needed to be trained to follow orders and commands without question. The authoritative style of coaching worked; it prepared young men for that purpose.

When the fighting was over and more athletic opportunities sprang up on the American landscape, authoritative style coaching was the norm. It was successful. Young men would run through walls because a coach would demand that of them. Coaches who attempted to use a more cooperative or holistic style of leadership were soft, laughed at, and often ridiculed.

Those coaches were scoffed at and accused of trying to be a "friend" or "wussifying" the young men. When Title IX became law, young women had opportunities to play sports. Males dominated the coaching profession, and it became necessary for them to embrace relationship building and strive for more balance. The authoritative coach could still be successful while coaching young women. However, coaches who embraced a style that focused on relationships found greater success as they worked with the female athlete. That success with female athletes and relationships started to show success with male athletes as well. This book will help you navigate a journey that will expose you to transformational coaching and mindfulness.

Mindfulness

The practice of maintaining a nonjudgmental state of heightened or complete awareness of one's thoughts, emotions, or experiences on a moment-to-moment basis also: such a state of awareness. (Webster)

To simplify, mindfulness is to *be present.* Your focus is on the task at hand, on those people that are around you. When you practice mindfulness with your family, you are not in front of a screen, your phone is off or away, you truly engage with those in the room.

Coaching for mindfulness is the latest buzzword in the leadership world. When we apply mindfulness to coaching athletics, we are attempting to teach our athletes to be fully aware of what is happening around them. As a high school football player, I had one job on every play. I had to know my responsibility for every call that came into the huddle. Our coach did not teach the game in a way that encouraged us to understand the duty of every other player on the field. We all had our jobs, and we had to make sure we did them.

When I went out for the school musical and learned I would be the lead role, I suddenly found out I had a lot of lines to learn. As my drama instructor worked with me, I soon found that I was learning everyone's lines. I was developing mindfulness without even realizing it. I had the lead role, so if someone forgot their line, I should know it. I learned that if I wanted the performance to be successful, part of my responsibility would be to help my cast.

When I returned to the gridiron the following fall, I became more aware of what the duties of my teammates were. Suddenly it was vital for me to know what routes players were running, whom they were blocking, who was a decoy, and what their missed block meant to me. The game suddenly opened up to me, and I became a more enlightened player.

If my football coach had had the tools to teach us how to play the game with mindfulness, the success of our football team would have reached unknown heights.

As an adult I found cycling to be my fitness pursuit of choice. Coaching can be stressful and healthy eating habits are often sacrificed for convenience. As my weight started to push up I told myself that cycling would affect the numbers I was seeing on the scale. I realized over some time that those numbers on the scale were not going in the direction I wanted, even with my cycling.

The problem was lack of mindfulness and lack of purpose; I was just riding. My eighty to one-hundred miles a week were just numbers. I didn't state my purpose, which was to lose weight. I didn't alter my diet, if anything I was eating a little more because I was exercising.

Mindfulness means to be present. State your purpose and then make sure your thoughts and actions reflect that purpose.

For those we coach, mindfulness also means to play without risk of ridicule when you make a decision based on how the game is being played. Coaches have a responsibility to create an environment where players are free to be creative and make in-moment game decisions.

Gratitude

The quality of being thankful; readiness to show appreciation for and to return kindness. (def.) I believe that players with a grateful attitude perform at a higher level. When we go to work, and we are thankful for the job we have and the money we earn, we attack the day with a positive attitude and perform at a higher level. When a player is upset because they are not in the starting line-up, it affects their practice performance. Their detrimental or lack-luster practice performance has that same effect on the team's performance that day. When the player comes to practice grateful for the opportunity to be part of that team and compete for a position or playing time, they work harder and find a way to help those around them improve. Having a grateful heart enhances the experience for everyone.

Mastery

Comprehensive knowledge or skill in a subject or accomplishment (def.) Mastery is something we strive for both as athletes and then as coaches. There may be a level of proficiency for an eight-year-old and then a new level as a nine-year-old. We may believe we achieved mastery as a senior high school basketball player; then, we have the opportunity to play in college. Collegiate basketball then presents a new level of proficiency.

Coaching/leading brings the same challenges. As I achieved mastery as a middle school wrestling coach, I had new areas to develop as I moved into the high school ranks. As a middle school coach, I had the highest participation numbers in the area. My athletes were motivated, they had a lot of success, and they were prepared to enter a high school program. I met all the expectations of a very successful coach at the middle school level.

As a high school coach, many of those same criteria were measurements of success, but now there were new levels of achievement for success and mastery. To achieve mastery, you must be a life-long learner.

Entitlement

The fact of having a right to something. The belief that one is inherently deserving of privileges or special treatment.

When you talk to coaches, teachers, employers, or business leaders, it will not take too long to hear the term entitlement dropped in the conversation. Coaches experience challenges with players, from the youth ranks to the professional level, that are rooted in entitlement. The player feels entitled to something. At the club level, they pay a lot of money; therefore, they are entitled to play. At the high school level, mom or dad dropped a considerable donation to the program, which entitles them to be the star player.

The player was all-state in high school, and therefore they are entitled to a starting position on their new college team. How many stories do we read about professional athletes who have signed a contract but sit out because they feel underpaid and entitled to more money? This belief causes issues between the player, the coach, and the team that can be corrected with transformational coaching.

The 2019 Dallas Cowboys looked to have a dynamite team coming into the season. On paper they had talented players on both sides of the ball. The team was destined to be the divisional champions and the fans were expecting a deep playoff run.

There were many reasons the team did not achieve the success that had been forecasted for them. I would argue that entitlement infected the team early and played a key role in them not meeting expectations.

Ezekiel Elliot, with two years to go on a five-year deal, decided he was worth more money and he would sit out the season until he got paid. Two other players, Amari Cooper and Zak Prescott, were in the final years of their contracts and neither appeared to be too worried about negotiations. Elliot's request now brought the other big contract players into the fray. Elliot's selfishness and me-first attitude started to cause rifts within the team. Whether the contract stress was real or fabricated, the only news was talk of the big three and how would Dallas be able to keep them all happy.

The team had lost their focus; they had lost their purpose. Jerry Jones, the owner, was talking a lot. Jason Garret, their coach was on the hot seat each week. There were too many distractions and even with all their talent, they could not put together enough wins. For Cowboy fans, the season was a disaster.

To reframe, with mindfulness you must clarify and state your purpose. Set checkpoints during the season to keep you mindful of your destination.

CHAPTER 1

The Youth Participation Crisis

"When they are not playing – they are not having fun. When they are not having fun – they quit."
–Unknown

Our youth sports participation numbers are dropping. According to The Sports & Fitness Industry Association (SFIA), youth participation has dropped from 45% to 37% in the past decade. The top three reasons: 1 Injuries, 2 Poor Coaching, 3 Cost.

More importantly, national statistics over the past decade have shown that between 70-75% of youth quit sports altogether by the time they reach the age of 13, prior to their freshman year of high school. In 2019, ESPN and the Aspen Institute launched a campaign to increase youth sport participation, called "Don't Retire Kid." Why are we seeing this trend?

Before we explore the reasons for the decline in youth participation, let us examine the history of the youth sports culture history. Massachusetts, in 1852, passed a law that made education mandatory. With school now taking up a big portion of the day, after school "free time" was now defined. Child-rearing experts of that time period believed that competitive sport leagues were in the best interest of children. In the beginning, that meant a push for playground and park development. Parents and other adults did not think it was best for young boys to be unsupervised so organized sports started to take root.

Our society was moving into the industrial age and sports were seen as the best arena to teach our country's values. Physical laborers were needed; hard work, cooperation, and respect for authority would be key attributes for employees at that time.

The New York City's Public School Athletic League for boys started in 1902. Elementary aged boys competed in track and field, basketball, and baseball. By 1914 they had city championships that were held in Madison Square Garden. Other cities saw the New York model and by 1910, 17 other cities formed their own athletic leagues. The boy's clubs that had formed were working with school leagues to expand across the country.

The depression hit, and many of these competitive clubs took a hit financially and were forced to close down. Many of the boys clubs/school programs dissolved, and poor kids lost out of adult organized sport activities. Organizations like the YMCA, started to offer programs that had a price tag attached. These groups provided the opportunities that were previously lost, but they started to price out the poorer children, and only children in the middle and upper classes were able to take advantage of these new programs.

During this time, many professional physical educators did not support athletic competition for these young boys. The club leagues focused on the best athletes and left many late-bloomers behind. The school programs no longer wanted to be involved with the club operations, and competitive athletics moved out of the elementary school system.

In 1929 Pop Warner Football started in Pennsylvania and came onto the scene. 1939 Little League Baseball began in Philadelphia, and they hosted the first Little League World Series in 1949. Then a self-esteem movement started in the 1960's and brought concerns to the elementary age child that competition at that age level was detrimental to student health and school performance. This attitude pushed more educational based athletic opportunities for youth to the club and for-profit programs. Parents still wanted competitive opportunities for their children, and they would spare no expense.

Parents of the 1960s spent a lot of their time with their children at sports practices and events; it was becoming part of our culture. AYSO

Soccer started their youth soccer program in 1964, originating in Los Angeles, and Biddy Basketball and Pee Wee Hockey programs started that year as well. Jump rope enthusiasts were not left out. In 1975, the American Double Dutch League started.

The 1990s brought more national organizations to the forefront. 1994 saw US Youth Soccer take off with the United States hosting the World Cup. In 1995, the Amateur Athletic Union sponsored close to 100 national championships for youth. By 2005 the AAU sponsored over 250 national athletic championships. USA Hockey began in 1999.

Let's now fast-forward to 2019 and take a look at the direction our youth sports culture is going, and then we will address the cost and the coaching pieces. Here is an example of the current youth timeline:

At ages 3 to 4, parents put their child in exploratory sport, dance, and movement classes. The child has fun, plays with a variety of balls, and meets other tiny people.

At ages 5 to 6, parents are exposed to "recreational" youth activities, i.e. t-ball, soccer, swimming, golf, hockey, to name a few.

At ages 7 to 10, parents and their children are starting to either examine or are being "recruited" for academy or select programs. The price for these activities start to skyrocket. Many parents have their kids in multiple activities to find the sport that their child is most proficient at.

During these ages, 3 to 10, the focus is on learning the skills of the game (development) and fun. Once the child transitions into the academy or select arena, fun and development are no longer the main focus, the priority becomes "winning." When winning becomes the priority at this early age, the loser is the child.

At ages 11 to 13, the child is starting to mature as a human and as an athlete. The late-bloomer is often pushed to the side or discarded during this stage. The tall and lanky 10-year-old is uncoordinated, slow, or both. A good coach will recognize this growth and maturity stage and stick with the child. The coach who is in a program or club that needs to produce wins will part ways with this child.

Because winning became the priority from ages 7 to 13, other factors come into play that will push kids into early retirement. When we put winning over development, the child that needs practice and opportunity to perfect their skills does not get enough time to master them and they fall behind their peers. When they fall behind, they make more mistakes. Those mistakes may put the team's chances of winning in jeopardy, and that takes away the playing time of that individual. When they are not playing - they are not having fun. When they are not having fun - they quit.

The player who falls behind starts to lose enjoyment of the game and becomes less involved in practice and other team activities outside of the game. The player who is allowed to develop and make mistakes becomes more creative and the game opens up to them. Unfortunately, we are losing many of those young players because programs that focus on grabbing the youth sports dollar think that winning is the carrot that draws the parents. This obviously is not working because 70% of our youth are retiring before their 14th birthday.

Cost

I remember being elected as the president of a youth soccer club in 1994. Our club had 350 children ages 6 to 19, and all but two teams registered as recreational teams. Our program had only one U12 and one U14 boys select team. Our registration fee was $35. In 1996 we had reached 1000 youth players, we had both boys and girls select teams at U12, U14, and U16. Our recreational fees jumped to $45, and our select fees were $90. By the year 2001 we had more than 1600 recreational players and 22 select teams, reaching a total of 2000 registered youth players. Our recreational fees were still $45 dollars and our select fees were $120. I left the club in 2014, our recreational fees had hit $85 and our select fees were $150.

Our club did a great job of keeping the costs affordable so that every child had an opportunity to play. That is not the story of others around the country, and was not the case of many programs within our state.

There were many programs in larger communities that had to deal with competing clubs and their fees were closer to $2000. The youth hockey team in our area had fees much higher than our soccer program, and the equipment costs were very high as well.

According to an article in Time magazine (August 24, 2017), kids' sports were a 15-billion-dollar industry in 2017. That number is a 55% increase since 2010, and it continues to grow. These numbers reflect travel, league registration fees, private coaching, apps that organize leagues and livestream games. There are marketing firms totally designed to help your child attract a college scholarship. Many colleges hold I.D. camps to attract players who think they have a shot at scholarship to that university. Many of these programs provide evaluation services, but the players they want have already been selected. What parents and players do not always understand is that only 2% of high school athletes go on to play for top level college sport teams.

Injuries & Sport Specialization

Another area of concern is the number of injuries that our youth are experiencing. Young players are leaving their games behind because of too many concussions, ACL tears, and shoulder surgeries. Many injuries are from overuse or trying to attend multiple practices during the same day. One study showed that athletes who participated in their primary sport for more than eight months of the year were more likely to report overuse injuries.

The following statistics can be found on the American Orthopedic Society's webpage, "Stop Sports Injuries":

1. According to the CDC, Center for Disease Control, over 30 million youth participate in sports across the US.
2. High school athletes account for over 2,000,000 injuries, 500,000 doctor-visits, and over 30,000 hospitalizations each year.
3. More than 3.5 million children under 14 receive medical treatment for a sport-related injury.

4. Children ages 5 to 14 account for about 40% of sports related injuries treated in hospitals.

The rising costs of participation is causing young athletes to pick a sport and specialize at too early of an age. Not only do their chances of injury increase, there is a higher risk of burnout and depression. Youth players need to be encouraged to participate in multiple sports through their mid-teens; it keeps their options open and if they are a late bloomer, so they don't give up before they blossom. A statistic that often gets ignored is that over 80% of Division 1 male and female athletes played an average of two to three sports as youth.

Coaching

Now the question becomes, "what can we do to help turn the tide?"

Coaching education is the key! As a high school coach, I have to take three online courses each year through the National Federation of High Schools. Those courses include: Concussions, Heat Illness, & Sudden Cardiac Arrest. My school requires CPR and First Aid every two years and a recruiting policy course every year. I provide this information because nationally only 30% of all coaches, club, youth, high school, recreational, receive any form of training. That same percentage receive education for skills, tactics, and conditioning.

Our youth programs would be stronger and provide more positive experiences if we could get all of our coaches trained within their sports. If coaches understood child development, they could make beneficial practice sessions to help foster their player's growth and enjoyment.

My college experience was in the early 80s, and my major was Education, specifically Physical Education, with an emphasis on coaching. Many colleges and universities offered a coaching emphasis or even a coaching minor. Unfortunately due to budget cuts, it is difficult to find a minor or an emphasis in coaching at the university level today.

There were not a lot of youth programs in the 80s, the coaching jobs were at middle schools, high schools, and colleges. Little league baseball and AAU basketball were around but many communities had limited middle school sports, and title IX had only passed in 1972, so athletic opportunities for girls, were in their infancy.

When people started learning the benefits and, more importantly, the financial impact of youth sport programs for children, the need for coaches skyrocketed. Moms and dads who played in high school were now begged to coach a youth team that their child played on. Club sports took off, and more and more parents were needed to coach all of the recreation and select teams in their local community. Some of these coaches were experienced, but even more were just filling a role and trying to get by.

These parents had no training, they were told to read a book or watch a video. The resources available today were not even heard of in the 90s and early 2000s. Many parents coached 8-year-olds the way they, the parent, were coached in high school. The parent who played for an authoritative coach in high school brought that intensity to a U8 practice. Once again, no training, no guidelines, those children did not have fun and often found other things to do.

I started out coaching high school wrestling, football, and track. When I graduated from college, I could not find any educational courses specific to coaching those sports. I did have the opportunity to attend coaching clinics in each of those sports. These sport conferences brought in successful coaches willing to share their knowledge. The presenters were not always selected on their ability to teach peers; they were brought in based on their success on the field. Some were good, while some of these speakers focused on their own accomplishments. Conferences today are professionally managed, and they provide valuable learning opportunities.

Like everything else, there was a cost to attend those conferences, and if there was a course to take, a cost to that as well. Money not only excludes kids from playing youth sports, it excludes coaches from taking those courses or attending clinics that will help them improve.

At the youth level, winning cannot be the focus. In order for a child to continue to play a game, the number one need is fun! Practices have to be meaningful and fun. When they participate in a game, everyone needs to play and be given an opportunity. If the program does not emphasize fun and development, the drop-out rate will be high. A coach that focuses on fun, and developing young players while not focusing on the scoreboard, will have a higher retention rate because they build relationships and praise the positives.

There is nothing wrong with bringing on a coach without any experience because you need a body, but there has to be a development plan in place for that coach. There also needs to be a good support system in place to help the coach when an issue arises that they are not yet prepared for.

The wheels have been set in motion; the focus on winning and getting that result is where our youth sports are heading. Parents will continue to pay for their child to be associated with success. The goal of this book is to better prepare our coaches, so even if they are hired into a "win-first culture", they will be able to add their touch to the team and allow kids to make mistakes and improve.

CHAPTER 2
Coaching Styles

"A coach will impact more people in a year than the average person does in a lifetime"
–Rev. Billy Graham

We think we can do it; how hard can it be? "It's just coaching a bunch of kids. When I was a player, I always thought I knew more than my coach, how hard can it really be?"

Let's take a look back and remember how or why we entered the coaching profession. Was coaching something you knew, at a young age, that you were destined to do? Maybe you were able to play at a post-secondary level, then decided to pursue a graduate assistantship following a familiar coaching path? You may have earned your first teaching contract and a sub-varsity coaching position was needed, so you filled it. Or maybe you were that parent or older sibling that stepped up to volunteer because your child or a younger brother/sister would not have had a team if the club didn't find a coach. Whatever the reason that pushed you to enter the coaching profession, I would imagine the conversation you would have with your younger self would offer a totally different perspective today.

It is easy for many non-coaches to sit in the stands or sit in front of the TV and have the answers for everything that is going wrong with the team they are watching. Those "armchair quarterbacks" do not see the discipline issues, the lack of effort, or the attitude issues that kids bring to practice each and every day. The common fan or parent isn't privy to the inside dealings of building a team. They can't begin to imagine the relationship building the coach has been orchestrating or the variety of other dynamics that go into who plays and who doesn't.

Parents and fans alike are always trying to figure out what the coach is all about. There are many different coaching styles, and while some will coach in a similar manner, no two coaches are the same. Most coaches will fall heavy into one category, but that doesn't prohibit them from utilizing pieces of different styles to fit the needs of their team.

When you study coaching styles, most experts will break it down to three distinct styles. As I examined the different styles, I believe we can identify four different categories of coaches: Autocratic, Democratic, Laissez Faire, and Transformational.

Autocratic: "It's my way or the highway!"

If I were a betting man, I would bet that everyone can name an example of a coach that fits this coaching style. This is often described as "the dictator" of the coaching profession. There is no room for questioning. This coach has procedures and policies in place, and the coach has absolute control. Players do exactly what the coach says, or they are off the team or riding the bench.

The autocratic coach is described as task-orientated. For decades this style of coaching was the norm. Many of us have played for coaches in this category. Autocratic coaches can be very successful, and as long as the win column is higher than the loss column, they are often free to continue to do the job. This style of coaching can be verbally abusive to players and has punishments built into poor performances or mediocre practices.

If we look back historically, the sport of football started at the high school level sometime in the late 19th century, and high school basketball started at a similar time in 1891. As the popularity of these two sports took off, our country was heading to WWI and then WWII. Following those wars, the Korean conflict and Vietnam followed.

Athletics became the training ground for future soldiers. We needed young men who would follow authority without question. Our soldiers were expected to follow those orders without question and be physically fit. Screaming at players, barking orders, punishment for mistakes, were tools to condition our kids for the real world, war and factory jobs.

This coaching practice carries on today. Many fathers played for coaches like this and believe this built character and kept their children in line. Task-oriented meant you have a job to do and there is no room for error. We see this coach often on the high school and college football and basketball sidelines. Players rotate through those programs every 2-3 years, and the community and the school know what they are getting. As long as the program succeeds, there are not a lot of outward complaints.

Many parents believe the coach is teaching discipline. Screaming and yelling at players is the norm, but to people outside the program it looks a lot like verbal abuse. Players who struggle under this coaching style are considered to be soft. If this coach is successful, many questionable behaviors that would normally not be tolerated are covered up or whitewashed over. When this coach is no longer winning, the things that are hidden in the dark come out in the light, and that coach's career is often over. The coach either moves on, is fired, or quits. Seldom do they reflect on the reasons. They blame soft kids and softer parents.

Democratic

This coach allows input from the players and assistant coaches. Players help determine rules and consequences. It allows more ownership, and the player becomes more of a stakeholder in the program.

When I started playing high school football, my coach, Doug Hjersjo, was the junior varsity coach, and due to a quick departure from our head coach, Coach Hjersjo took over our varsity program. It was obvious that Coach Hjersjo was brought up playing in an autocratic program, and there were moments where that style would surface.

As a sophomore, starting on the varsity, I experienced my only season without winning a game, as a player or a coach. The transition to a new coach within the first two-weeks of the season and a disgruntled senior class were deep issues within the team, the outcome - we struggled. Coach Hjersjo would come in at half-time. We were usually down by at least a touchdown, and he would blow a gasket. We had a steel shopping cart in the locker room for towels, and he would grab that cart and smash it into a support beam in the middle of the room.

That action was supposed to grab our attention and fire us up. Sorry coach, but that wasn't the effect. We were screamed at, we went out after halftime, and just gave up more points.

As that group of seniors left, Coach Hjersjo started to show his real style, and he was more of a democratic coach. We had a voice as players and he allowed us to have input into our season. I would even go so far as to say that he was leaning towards transformational decades before that became a thing. Coach Hjersjo was eventually inducted into Wisconsin High School Football Coaches Hall of fame.

Laissez Faire: Often described as a player's coach.

This coach is laid back, and nothing appears to raise their blood pressure. This coach may have discipline issues if the players think they can do whatever they wish. Often young coaches take on a submissive style of coaching. This coach is not too far removed from playing the game, and they are still close in age to their players. They can relate to them on a different level and need to remember to keep some boundaries. The submissive coach may try to be more like a friend because they want the athletes to like them. They often do not enforce rules, and there is no discipline for poor behavior during a game. They may even become involved in trash talking from the sidelines themselves.

The team is often undisciplined and eventually the coach loses the team. When the coach loses control of the team, coaching becomes stressful, problems come to the forefront, and the coach is often let go or they quit on their own. Those coaches that really want to continue will often start over as an assistant with another team and improve their techniques or look to further educate themselves with training.

There are also coaches that discover during this stage that they can find a balance between being task-orientated and laissez faire.

Transformational

At one time this style may have been called holistic coaching. Transformational coaching emphasizes life lessons within the sport the athlete is participating in. Everyone from parents to players feel like they are a valuable part of the program. A transformational coach will stress character traits and values as important cornerstones for success.

Transformational coaching places the player and their development on and off the field as the main focus. Transformational coaches know that athletes with good character will perform better on the field and in the classroom. In order to coach this way, the coach needs to be aware that they are always modeling the behaviors they want their players to exhibit. The quote, "what you do is always louder than what you say", is important to remember as you take the transformational path.

A transformational coach needs to be aware of the effects of emotion on the team. Not only the emotions of the players but their own emotions. When I started coaching at the varsity level, there was an experienced coach we would play against who I believed practiced many unethical behaviors. The play of his team, the actions he demonstrated and the expectations he had of his team did not fall in line with sportsmanship and fair play.

His interactions with his players, his interactions during competition with my players, and his interaction with me was not appropriate and was always intended to intimidate. The first few years, his teams were better than we were. When I reflect back, I wonder how much did my own actions affect my team's performance. The intimidation tactics this coach used had an effect on me. Even though I tried to hide it, I am sure that my actions were louder than anything I said.

I have passion for the game, and I want my players to channel their own passion. Passion is defined as a barely controllable emotion. If it is barely controllable, and we want our players to have passion, then we must also teach them how to control their passion.

One of the ways to teach them to control emotion is to model it as the coach. Examine your behavior when a player makes a mistake. What message does the team receive from you? How do respond when your team gives up a goal, a basket, a score? Do you yell at the player who made the error? Your players on the bench are watching your behavior at all times. Are you supportive or instructive, or do you substitute and chastise?

There may be a time where a display of emotion fires up the team or lets them know that you have their back, but that display must be controlled. If you succumb to emotion, you can say or do something that will have a detrimental effect on what you are trying to teach. When your players react with emotion, there is usually a negative team consequence; taking the time to address this can go a long way.

Transformational coaching prioritizes relationship development. Another of my favorite quotes states that: "Players don't care how much you know; they want to know how much you care." The thinking is that if you don't build meaningful relationships with your team, they will never lay it all on the line for you. Just think back to your own playing experience. Did you play harder when you were afraid of your coach or when you had a relationship with them? My personality had me giving my best effort all of the time; however, when I knew my coach really cared about me, I didn't ever want to let them down.

I make it a point to know who my players are dating, where they work, and if they hold down a job. I want to know if they have siblings, and/or if their grandma and grandpa are coming to the game. It helps to know what they are involved with in school and what classes they are struggling with. They appreciate when you take the time to ask about something other than the sport they play for you.

My teams have always had character values that we want to emulate. Instead of focusing on rules, we look at 4-6 character values and make them part of our program. What does responsibility look like, not only on the playing field but in the classroom, at home, in the community, and within the team? Our program has a code of conduct. Being responsible is following that code. I don't need to add more rules.

When a player has a setback, we address the issue as it relates to our core values. Relating the incident to our core keeps it from becoming the coach yelling at the player for a mishap, but we focus on making it a learning experience. We teach the core values throughout the season and throw in other traits as we move through the season.

Transformational coaches are now the leaders in making mindfulness a part of their player's development. Let's take a deeper look at what coaching mindfulness looks like in the next chapter.

CHAPTER 3
Mindfulness

"You cannot control the results, only your actions."
-Allan Lokos

Mindfulness is a term often spoken in the world of yoga and meditation. More recently the business world is adopting the mindfulness mantra. It is only fitting that we, in the coaching world, adopt this concept and find a way to incorporate mindfulness into our leadership tool kit. We will be able to challenge our teams and lead them to higher levels of success if we can get them to be present – to be mindful. Coaches do not have to be Zen masters.

True meditational mindfulness is about being "in the moment," the ability to focus in on what you are doing and being in control of your emotions. Novak Djokovic, Serbian professional tennis player, uses mindfulness techniques to be a better tennis player. Novak no longer plays tennis to *prove* himself; he uses tennis to *improve* himself and those around him. When we practice mindfulness we are teaching our players to focus on their actions and what they need to do to make the shot or their pass successfully. We are providing a tool for them to focus on their performance and not let emotion affect that performance.

Let's go to the tennis court. You faulted on your first serve. Now you have another chance, so what are you focusing on? Are you mad that you missed it? Is your self-talk screaming at you for making a mistake? When we are present in the moment (mindful), we are thinking about the serve itself. We are not thinking about rushing the net or where we are going after the serve. We are thinking about a high toss, keeping our head up, and the hit. What do I need to do right now to get the ball in play?

As we begin to include mindfulness into our coaching, we start looking at the big picture. We want our athletes to be focused on our team, what our game plan is, what our goals are. We want them to be present each and every day. We want them to understand how all of the puzzle pieces fit together.

As an athlete participating in high school athletics in the late 70's, I was coached to do my job. As a running back in football, I knew when to carry out a fake, where to run when I was handed the ball, and who to block when the play called for it. As a wrestler, I was drilled to set up moves and attack, drilled counter measures when my opponent tried something, and was conditioned to outlast everyone. As a track athlete, it was also just go on the gun, run as hard as I could, and get myself across the finish line. I was not coached to know what my teammates' responsibilities were. As I look back on those early years, I was quite clueless.

My first experience with mindfulness, long before mindfulness was a "thing", was during my drama experience in high school. As a naive freshman boy, I earned the leading role in my first high school musical. It was during the preparation and rehearsal for our production that I learned what mindfulness, being self-aware, was all about.

As the lead role, the play was centered around my character, yet for the performance to be memorable and highly reviewed, everyone had to be present. Every cast and crew member needed to know the roles and lines before and after theirs. The lead will have the most lines, and if someone forgets a line or misses a cue, there are people in place to help remind them. As the lead, I knew everyone's lines and how everyone's actions affected the overall performance.

It took a little longer for me in the athletic arena. I was used to being told where to go and what to do. There was no room for improvisation. We were not coached why we were running a particular play or how we were really a decoy on the route, or how we were testing our opponent.

Coaching training and coaching education was limited to some colleges that may have offered a few classes. There were not organizations that specialized in providing that tool. There were no online opportunities to develop as a coach. The coaching knowledge someone had was limited to what they were exposed to as a player. Coaches mimicked the style of the men or women who coached them in high school or college.

As we train our players and make practice sessions more competitive, we start to learn more about our players, and our players learn more about their teammates. When we know a player's tendencies when they get stressed, we can anticipate them and not allow the moment to hurt the team. The team becomes stronger because we know our strengths and weaknesses.

Being mindful makes us aware of parental expectations and feelings, opening lines of communication and enhancing the parents' experience with the team. Transformational coaches realize that we can no longer just coach the players on our roster; they have to coach the parents, often the administration, and even a community. If you want to survive, even excel in the profession, the job of a coach has become that much more complex. With greater complexity also comes greater rewards.

Mindfulness is when you are being fully present. How often do you think your players are fully present in practice? How many times do you believe they are fully present in games? How many times do you put a drill together for teenage boys, and as soon as you turn to work with another group, the drill breaks down and the boys are doing their own thing. That is an example of your team not being fully present, they are not working to accomplish what you laid out before them. While they may be getting some practice with whatever skill or tactic is involved in the drill, they are missing the "big picture" of how it relates to the game.

Mindfulness is being aware of everything around us. For your athletes that means they are paying attention to not only their responsibility but also how the opponent is reacting to your play. Your players are recognizing their opponent's tendencies and weaknesses, and they can use that knowledge to gain an advantage. Coach A puts in a player that cannot dribble the basketball to the right, or does not have much control with the left hand. A team that can recognize that early can expose it and make the game easier.

Mindfulness is not being over-reactive. A coach that trains the team to respond to any setback can rebound and show resilience. A team that collapses when something bad happens is not in control of their emotions and lacks confidence to compete.

Coaches can put their teams in different situations in practice to help prepare them for anything that can happen in a game. Even greater learning takes place when the coach doesn't provide the answer to problems but allows the players to figure them out. This is transformational coaching. This is coaching with mindfulness.

Bringing mindfulness into your daily training will be a shift in the way you train your team. You will have to change the mindset of your team. You are now asking young players to process your training sessions instead of just performing. You are going to be engaging the players on more cerebral level to benefit the physical efforts they put in. A great way to make this transition is through a Yoga experience. At the beginning of your new season, schedule a session with a local instructor. If they have a place of business, schedule a team session away from the regular practice site. Depending on the size of your team, you may want to schedule more than one to keep the group manageable. The yoga instructor must be able to work with the age-group you are coaching; it may take a few minutes for the group to settle in. Dealing with maturity can be a challenge if the instructor is not familiar with that age group, especially boys.

One introductory session with a good instructor will help you move mindfulness into your coaching sessions. After our team yoga session, we were able to calm ourselves by using breathing techniques and focusing on our task. We were able to take the last moments of a practice session, close our eyes, focus on our breathing, and reflect on our training, or prepare for our next opponent. Our yoga experience, with a trained instructor, helped us accelerate our move to more mindfulness as a team.

CHAPTER 4

The Mindfulness Brain

"Educating the mind without educating the heart is no education at all."
–Aristotle

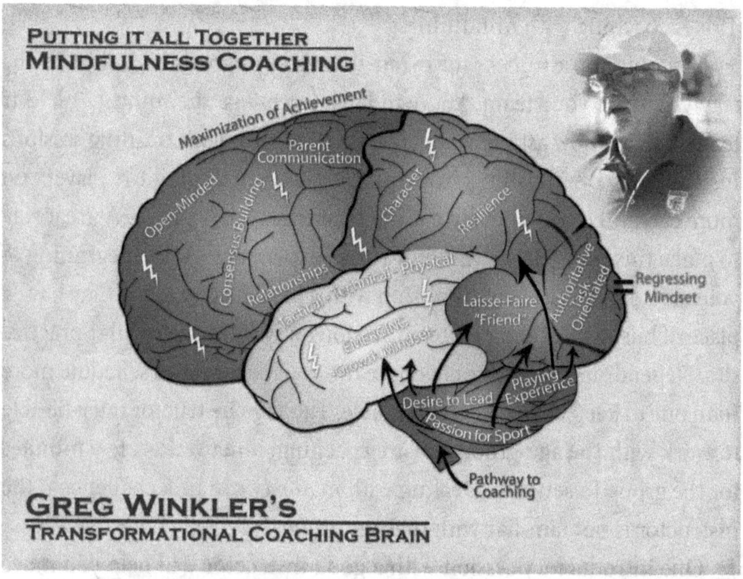

I often start coaching seminars with the question, "What is your WHY?" It is important to reflect back on why you chose to enter into this often thankless profession. Some began because they were fulfilling a volunteer commitment while others believe they had a calling or were destined to coach. Whatever your "why," it is valuable to reflect on your reason and remind yourself why you started your coaching career.

Because we are talking about mindfulness, what better representation than the use of the brain or the mind. Most coaches, regardless of the sport, are familiar with John Wooden's Pyramid of Success. Wooden's pyramid of success represents basic needs that must be met for the player to move up to a more sophisticated level. The completion of each level leads towards mastery as an athlete.

My "Brain" example is different. All of the areas that you see in this brain are important for a mindful and transformational coach. Unlike Wooden's pyramid, a coach can be successful even if they ignore some of the areas identified. If your only definition of success is the win/loss column, you can put this book away right now. If your "why" as a coach included molding young men and women into responsible citizens of the community and if you believe relationships are essential for success, then this brain diagram will help you.

We will remember the relationships we developed with our team and our coaches long after we forget our win/loss record. Let's use this "Brain" diagram to see if we can become a coach of mindfulness.

We will use the brain stem as our path of entry. I have identified three experiential triggers that push us to the coaching pathway. They include: Previous playing experience, passion for a sport, a strong desire to lead or give back to a game that influenced you.

Participation in an activity, a sport, or a game is how most people develop a desire to coach. They may have had success in the game they played, or they had a great experience and developed meaningful relationships. My high school football experience, from a win/loss perspective, was dismal. My three-year varsity career netted a win/loss record of 7-20. It was the relationship that I had with the coach and the connection I made with my teammates that pushed me toward coaching.

After football season, I hit the wrestling mat. Once again I was blessed with a coach of character, by the name of Dave Moon. Coach Moon expected the best out of us but also let us know that he genuinely cared about us as individuals. Coach Moon took over a mediocre program and put us on a path to success.

When the winter sport ended, I hit the track, exposing me to a new coach and a different coaching style. Coach Peters coached the cross-country team in the fall and had many of his runners on the track team. Despite my performances and efforts to impress him, his loyalty went to his cross-country runners. He wanted me to quit football and join the cross-country team; because I continued with football, our relationship was never what it could've been. I learned lessons from Coach Peters that would benefit me in the future as I started dealing with athletes on my own teams.

My high school coaches had a significant impact on my life as a teenager. They knew how to build relationships yet hold the players accountable. I saw the effect they had on every player on the team. These men presented a caring and calming presence to young men and women as they navigated adolescence. I wanted to be that person for young athletes.

We do not always have to come into coaching from playing the game. I know of coaching organizations that miss out on some great coaches because they believe you have to have played the game to teach it. Although many coaches have proven that thinking false, they continue to bypass good candidates. My coaching legacy has been built on the soccer pitch. A sport I only played in a physical education class and a brief stint in an adult recreation league.

We have entered the brain through whatever path we chose. Now the real work begins.

The Path to Burnout or a Regressive Mindset

If we come into the profession with a background that leans towards authoritative or task-oriented coaching, we may be on our way out quickly. We discussed this method earlier and learned that without a desire to improve in our craft, we could get stuck here, and if not successful, we may be leaving the profession before we even get started.

The submissive coaching style or laissez-faire coach, without a sound support system or educational path for growth, will struggle. That coach may also find themselves giving up on the profession. Without discipline, success is hard to come by.

Following either of these two pathways puts us in an area of the brain that is soon closed off to the rest. These coaches become entrenched in a regressive mindset. Instead of working to enhance their coaching toolbox, they stay in the same place, and because others around them are moving forward, their attitude about coaching has them going backward.

When a coach is reluctant to learn from others, the lack of growth starts to form a thick wall around that part of the brain, and they get trapped. It is like they had a brain injury, and they lose access to the great things they are capable of learning.

Emerging – Having a Growth Mindset

If we are looking to be "emerging" or prominent in our field, having a growth mindset is a character trait we need to develop. A growth mindset is required to maximize achievement. A growth mindset is characterized as a love of learning. Ask yourself, how many coaching books have I read? What sports journals do I read? How many online activities have I bookmarked? Do you prefer books or articles that deal with your sport, or do you look to coaches of other sports for inspiration and knowledge? What coaching or sports organizations do you belong to?

When you are an emerging coach, these questions are easy to answer. If you want to maximize your achievement in your chosen field, these questions can be a guide of where to look. I do not coach football or basketball anymore. Many of those coaches have written the best coaching leadership books. It would be foolish of me not to read them because my sport is different.

Joe Ehrmann wrote a great book on transformational coaching, "Inside Out Coaching." He is an ex-football player turned lacrosse coach. If I ignore his book because I don't like football or lacrosse, then I would be missing out on an opportunity for growth. Tony DiCicco wrote a great book on coaching youth, and he was a soccer coach. I would miss out on a great book about coaching youth if I didn't pick it up because it had a soccer ball on the cover.

A coach has the opportunity to learn and grow, not only from those that are successful in the same sport. Many coaching strategies can be utilized in every area of life. There are many books by successful business leaders that can improve your athletic coaching, and likewise, business leaders can learn much about leading by emulating successful coaching styles.

The Nuts and Bolts of Your Game

To be successful, you must be aware and keep up with the best practices of your game. You will not survive very long in your field if you are not knowledgeable about the technical, tactical, and physical requirements of your game. Real coaching comes in if you can teach and how you teach your players the nuts and bolts of your game.

Part of the challenge is making your instruction relatable to the age of the child you are coaching. Teaching the pick and roll to 7-year-olds will cause you to tear your hair out. A 7-year-old is aware of themselves and the ball they're using but nothing else! Focusing your efforts on dribbling and shooting a lay-up will provide the player more success and greater satisfaction. Coaches should read up on child development and understand what developmental level a child is at as they prepare their practice session.

I watched a friend, Brian, coach his 7-year-old son in t-ball. Brian's father, Mike, was the assistant coach for this little t-ball team. Mike, now the 7-year-old's grandfather, coached Brian in many sports as he grew up. Brian is 6'7", he grew slowly and was always coordinated and ahead at his age. Brian excelled at every game he picked up and eventually played college basketball. Fast-forward to today, Brian has a young boy that will be extremely tall; unlike his dad, this young 7-year-old is already as tall as many middle school boys. His coordination and balance are not able to keep up with his growth spurts, making him awkward and lanky.

As a coach, you can picture this young boy. Anyone who has coached young players, see this all the time. This young man will eventually fill in and catch up with his growth spurts. A coach with a background in child development will have patience with this young athlete, knowing they may not see the rewards of their coaching until this boy reaches high school. Without this knowledge, the child may be scolded and not feel they are doing a good job. This will be a blow to their confidence or self-esteem at age 7, leading them to choose another activity.

Many of our youth coaches have no coaching education in their background. Coaches may not be familiar with child development, and they will coach an 8-year-old the same as they would a teenager. Many youth coaches will only be concerned about "winning," even at the t-ball level. Children that play for coaches like this will lose interest and may leave the playing field very early in their development.

Not fully understanding child development is where Mike gets frustrated. He expects his grandson to be the athlete that his son was at that age. Mike has to work very hard not to show his frustration and his disappointment when this tall 7-year-old grandson makes mistakes as he is trying to manipulate his body to learn these new skills. He has to remind himself of the outcome that we want with 7-year-olds playing t-ball. Like any youth sport, the expected result at the end of the season should be that the players "love" the game.

Hopefully, they got a little better throughout this experience, but if they learned to love the game, they would continue to practice and to play that game. The goal would be to develop an interest in the game that will last for years instead of having a "one-hit-wonder."

Communication and Getting the Parents Involved

Mindfulness in coaching can influence every area of this brain diagram and create synergy. How do we teach character and still have time to develop the skills needed to play the game? A coach that seeks a growth mindset wants to communicate with parents, wants to work at building relationships, and produce quality practice plans. Such a coach may easily feel overwhelmed. How can we do it all? It is challenging!

A good coach is an excellent teacher. A good coach is an excellent communicator. Coaching requires not only demonstrating a new technique but more importantly, showing why the technique is effective. As we teach a new tactic, we don't just say "do it this way," we communicate why we do it this way, what impact it has within the team, and how it affects the opponent. Allowing the players to ask questions and having the answers for them is crucial for their understanding and buy-in. When I ask why, and the answer is, "because you said so," that is not good enough anymore. Players want to know the purpose of the activity. By not providing the purpose you become an autocratic coach, not transformational.

Parents can be your biggest supporters or your biggest obstacles. Communicating your philosophy and your expectations can help you avoid potential problems or misunderstandings during the season. With excellent communication, you can make the parents feel part of the experience. You are not just coaching the players, you are coaching the family.

Many years ago, I put together a club team of 9-year-olds and moved them to the select U-11 competitive level. Playing up is a common practice today, but when I put this team together and made this move, there were not very many teams taking that risk. Developmentally, my players needed more competition than our local recreation league provided, and the select league offered three levels of play.

As their coach, results were not important to me, the chance for the team to push themselves as players became the focus of that season. The challenge was whether the parents would support this venture even when the results on the scoreboard were not favorable. My challenge was "setting the narrative" and teaching the parents what to look for as they watched our contests.

On the scoreboard, we finished just below a .500 season. The challenges we faced and the growth we gained showed up years later as this group entered high school. There were outcomes that we looked for each game; those outcomes (goals) were communicated with the parents, and evaluating those after each game became our scoreboard. We had an enjoyable season and probably experienced the most significant growth as a group during that season. If the communication between coach and parent, even player and coach, weren't effective, the experiment probably would have failed.

Author, Stephen Covey, *The 7 Habits*, says, "Begin with the end in mind." Knowing what your end game is, will help guide your coaching and its effectiveness.

CHAPTER 5
Preparing to Lead

"The ultimate leader is one who is willing to develop people to the point that they eventually surpass him or her in knowledge and ability."
–Fred A. Manske Jr.

Coaching is leadership. The Oxford dictionary defines leadership as: the action of leading a group of people or an organization.

You are now a coach. Whether you are leading a group of six-year olds or group of young men or women, you are their guide, their leader. Not only are you leading them, you are leading those that support them. For example, if you are the coach of a high school varsity volleyball team, not only are you leading the athletes on your squad, you are leading the junior programs and those coaches below you. The position may provide a voice for you with the communities' youth programs. You could now be a leader to all of them. You are also the leader for the parents of the athletes in your program. You may not have realized it when you accepted the position, but you influence more than just the athletes on your squad.

At a recent leadership conference I attended, Dr. Henry Peel of Florida SouthWestern College provided the group with some leadership questions to answer. As I looked over the questions, I modified them a little to make them directly relatable to a coach in the athletic field. We will look at these through the transformational coaching lens.

So now you are a head coach, what is different about your position?

Congratulations. The program is now in your hands. Maybe you earned this position by working your way up through the ranks as an assistant coach. Maybe you happened to jump right into a head coaching position. The reality will hit! Everything that you may have taken for granted before is now under your direction. I will not use the word "control" because we are looking at this from the transformational view. You may be allowed to have a voice on hiring your staff. If you do get to pick a staff, do it carefully. We will address some of this in the question about job descriptions.

If you inherit a staff, your responsibility will be to lay out your mission, your coaching style, and expectations. As the head coach, you have the opportunity to "set the narrative" with your team, the parents, and with those that administer over you.

You are now the leader, the voice and the face of the program. You will be the model; you need to be prepared to "walk the talk."

Should your players be involved in decision making?

You have committed to being a transformational leader. Therefore, you see the value in including your team in the decision-making process. Why? If you give your athletes a voice, you are creating stake-holders within the team. Some coaches fear that they are giving away some of their power or control, but in reality the team becomes stronger because players now have a stake in the outcome.

As the coach, you do not have to solicit decisions from your players on everything. You choose where you can provide those decision-making opportunities for them. When setting up team rules or curfews, you can provide options for the team to discuss and collaborate on. A survey could be given to the team to encourage dialogue. The key here is that you, the coach, are allowing input but also providing options that you can live with.

Maybe you're a football coach and you have a list of plays you like to run in the red zone. Allow the players to have input on which ones they like the best. Then focus on running those plays. This method will be a confidence builder for the team and pay off when you need it. The team bought in and will be motivated to prove they can succeed.

When I was a high school senior, I was the tailback on our football team. It was the final game of the season, and the game was almost over. We had a comfortable lead, and I was 30 yards away from our school record for rushing yards. I had no idea I was that close. I bugged my coach all season about throwing a half-back option pass (we all want to be a quarterback). We were 34 yards away from the end zone, and Coach Hjersjo called me over and asked me if I wanted to have the next few carries and break the school record for rushing yards, or I could fulfill my dream of throwing the option pass.

I chose the option pass. We ran the play, I rolled to the right, saw my wide receiver Tim Navis camping out in the end zone. I fired a laser to him standing there waiting in the end zone. To be honest, the pass looked more like a wobbly punt. Tim almost did a fair catch in the end zone. Fortunately, he caught my pass and we scored. That is one of the only plays I actually remember from my glory days.

Coach Hjersjo did not have to call that play, he did not even have to put me back in the game, but he knew that play would be something I would remember forever. We were a .500 football team; we worked hard, and we had fun. Coach Hjersjo helped turn our culture around during his time, and as athletes we became better people because of him.

Remember, when you allow players to have input on some of the team decisions, you are making them stakeholders. You are not giving up power; you are making the unit stronger. You are helping to create memorable lifelong experiences.

What is the importance of flexibility? What is the downside?

What are you really teaching your players when you show flexibility? My life attitude is "go with the flow." I teach physical education at a high school without a gym. It's Southwest Florida, so it is always nice and seldom ever rains. My classes are always outside. I may be in the middle of class and a storm pops up and lightning is detected. I have to immediately take my students inside, the lesson I planned has now changed. For many teachers this sudden change could throw off their entire day and cause them much unneeded stress. Students easily pick up on a teacher's stress, which in turn causes the teacher even more stress. Keeping a calm presence, a "go with the flow" attitude helps students learn that conflicts will always arise and we can handle them. There is always an alternative.

The teams I coach and the students I teach learn that when you encounter an obstacle, there is no need to panic. We will work together to find another way to attack the issue. At just about every school across the country, practice space and time becomes an issue within the athletic department. An example would be during the high school basketball season. The boys and girls compete at the same time of the year. Each program may have 2 or 3 teams that include a varsity, junior varsity, and possible freshman program.

Both programs may want to practice right after school, but there is limited gym space, and having all teams practice at once is not possible. Maybe there is an alternate site that works, but one program has to travel. The athletic director has to work with both head coaches and come up with a plan that works. This is not an easy issue. There may be travel involved, and players may have jobs that need to allow them to come in to work later if they practice right after school. Coaches may have personal or family issues that require them to have a set time.

It is hard to get a win-win when multiple teams and personalities get involved. Coaches need to ask for fairness, yet remember to pick their battles. Having an open mind may actually open you up to a better situation.

Our boys' and girls' soccer teams both want to practice after school. When we start the season we have one game field that is available for practice. The previous season, the girl's coach wanted to do a late practice, so the boys went right after school and the girls followed. Both coaches practiced when they wanted to.

The following year, the girl's coach wanted to switch practice times. That became a problem as many of the boys had jobs for the evening, and the only workable time was after school. The boy's program could have complained and demanded equal time, instead they looked for an alternative.

There are county fields not too far from the high school. The county fields are maintained by the local club, there are bathrooms there, and available storage space. The boy's program worked with the club and changed sites. The switch worked out great and the boys came out better in the long run. It was because they were flexible and willing to look to find another way to attack an issue.

Can you be too flexible? Obviously, if issues present themselves and you are the one always giving in, that is not healthy either. Your team and your parents may see this as a weakness and you may lose some of your credibility. It is up to you to examine the issue. Examine the request, is it fair? Is there an opportunity to add value your program? In the end, being flexible and being able to adapt to changes shows your team that when obstacles arise, we don't panic and we look for positives in every situation.

What is the importance of job descriptions? Can they be a hindrance?

What does a job description have to do with coaching? There are two areas we are going to address with job descriptions: player roles and assistant coaches. Let's start with our players.

For our players, a job description could cover attendance requirements, academic expectations, as well as the rules or guidelines they are expected to follow to be a member of your team. Then you can have job descriptions for the position they expect to play. There are different requirements or expectations for a power forward on your basketball team compared to your shooting guard. A job description explains the requirements of the position to the player. It can describe the physical and mental demands needed to be successful and can be a guide for their off-season development.

If we are adding mindfulness to our coaching practice, players should know the job description of every position on the team. In game mindfulness, means that when a teammate gets out of position, everyone knows what that player's responsibilities are and can help until they get back into play. For the player that just got out of position, they recognize a teammate is covering for them and take on that role until they team can reset.

Having a job description for your assistant coach is extremely important. As the leader of your program, it is essential that your assistants know what you expect of them. The more details you add, the easier it becomes to hold them accountable. If you have an expectation and your assistant does not know about it, you will become frustrated.

When I took over a new head coaching position, I inherited an assistant/junior varsity coach. We had a coaches meeting, we discussed expectations, and I got him on board with the goals of the program. There was no written job description and no agreement to sign.

As the season wore on, my assistant wasn't on the sideline with me during varsity games. He did not show up to team functions and he would be late to his junior varsity practices. I felt like I did not have an assistant. It was very frustrating, and it was my own fault. I had to make a change after the season and before I hired a replacement, I created the job description for the assistant coach.

Just like the job description I had for my players, I included practice times, attendance requirements, and expectations of a coach. When creating the description always include more than what is actually required, it is always easier to eliminate items then to add them later.

What does "own the problem" mean?

What happens when there is an issue with your team? You are the leader, you have worked on being a transformational coach, what do you do now? As the coach, you own it! Publically you accept the criticism. You take the blame (if there is any), if there is a problem, that means you or your team made a mistake. What do you do when your players make mistakes? Do you assign blame or do you look at mistakes as an opportunity for growth?

Players will only get better or make changes if they try new skills or new tactics. When they try and they are not successful, it is classified as a mistake. When you look at a mistake as an opportunity to learn, you can fix the "problem", and you can grow as a team.

Once you realize you have a "problem" and you have decided to "own it", the next step would be to get the team together and address the issue. It may be that because of your experience you already know how you want to attack the issue, but you want stakeholders, so you bring it to the team, and you ask them for input.

Who should get credit for success?

You have read enough of this book already that this should be an easy question to answer. Your team should always get credit! When you win, all accolades should go to the players. When you lose, the coach owns the loss.

Are post-season evaluations effective?

I will write up a post-season evaluation for my returning players. The evaluation will highlight their strengths over the course of the season and what they can work on to improve providing them the opportunity for greater production in the next season.

The negative to a post-season evaluation would be if it was the only feedback a player received throughout the season. Your players should be receiving daily feedback and post-performance feedback. A player can make great strides in development over the course of the season if they receive specific and immediate feedback.

Reflect for a moment on how you like feedback. When your administrator questions something you are doing, are you receptive or do you feel attacked? Would you prefer frequent positives or just wait until your post-season evaluation. We are no different than our athletes. We want to be the best we can as a coach or a teacher. If there is an area that I can improve in, I would like to know immediately. I do not want to wait four or five months for an exit interview. Your players deserve the same thing. To help motivate your players, communicate and praise often.

So yes, post-season evaluations are effective, but daily feedback and support will provide your players with greater growth.

What do you think of telling someone "Good Job?"

Good job Greg! "Thanks I know, wait - what for?"

It is always nice to hear from someone that you did a good job, but was it meaningful? Coaching experts will tell you that you should provide positive feedback to criticism at a 7:1 to 11:1 ratio. Saying good job alone should not count as one of the positive tallies. Positive feedback should be specific, which makes it more meaningful.

Many football coaches have reward helmet stickers for player achievement during games. Tackle for a loss – sticker; 100 yards rushing for the offensive line – sticker; defensive interception – sticker. These are "good job" awards for game performance, and the team celebrates them. The standard was set and a public display of recognition is accepted.

I am talking about the effort in conditioning. Making the right decision to pass instead of shoot in basketball practice and cleaning up the practice area when everyone has left. We say good job, often it is implied what it was for, but when we specify the reason, the compliment is more meaningful.

"Sophia, thank you for cleaning up the water bottles after practice. We are trying to practice respect and you just showed a respect for our field and environment by cleaning up after your teammates. Good job"

"Rocco, that decision you made to run that overlap opened up space for Oliver to get open in front of the net and score that goal. Good job."

Specific, meaningful feedback makes the player feel recognized and reinforces a behavior you want to continue.

"Focus on outcomes, not process." What does this mean?

The buzzword on many professional teams lately has been "trust the process", so why are you telling me to focus on the outcomes?

Outcomes are different than results. When we are results orientated, we fall into the autocratic coaching style, the complete opposite of transformational coaching. You can set outcome goals for every training session. Explain what it is you want to accomplish today. When the practice session is over, a quick wrap up at the end can provide feedback and can help determine if your goal for the day, the outcome of the practice, was accomplished.

When I think of the "process," I think of the journey through the entire season. The team makes goals at the beginning of the year, and there is a process over the course of the season to achieve them. Your "outcomes" are your short-term goals established each day to reach your long-term goal. The process was that journey.

Can communication be active at all organizational levels?

Communication is the key to success and survival as a coach. If you aren't "setting the narrative" and providing information to your parents and administration, someone else will. In our program we use every form of communication we can. We have social media pages for our team to get the attention of those that use those avenues. We use a communication app that families and players can sign up and follow us.

We do a bi-weekly newsletter that we email, blast on social media, and share with our sponsors. There is no reason for anyone to say that they did not receive the information about what the team was doing.

I have mentioned "setting the narrative" a few times. Let me give you an example of what that looks like. When we send our newsletter out during the season, it includes a recap of every game played in that time period. We had played a very tough opponent, we played poorly, the team we played displayed tactics that were not within the guidelines of good sportsmanship. We did not respond appropriately and not only lost badly, we lost our composure.

It was embarrassing to our coaching staff and not the direction we wanted our program to go. We went back to practice the next day and we "owned the problem." Our parents were focusing on the behavior of our opponent. I learned, as the new coach, that there have been issues in the past with this team, and the relationship between the two communities was not a positive one.

In my game recap, I took responsibility for not having my team properly prepared. I reemphasized what our core values were as a team and how we, under my direction, did not demonstrate that value. We took the blame off the opponent and owned our actions. We played the team at home a few weeks later. Our parents were great hosts, and we did not react to their tactics. Our emotional control frustrated our opponent even more, causing the exact opposite reaction from the first game. Our opponent lost control, which led to a couple ejections for their team, and we beat them for the first time in program history.

You cannot "over-communicate," and communicating your message is another avenue to educate you parents and administration.

CHAPTER 6
Start With a Growth Mindset

"If you find a path with no obstacles,
It probably doesn't lead anywhere."
–Frank A. Clark

Growth Mindset: "In a growth mindset, people believe that their most basic abilities can be developed through dedication and hard work—brains and talent are just the starting point. This view creates a love of learning and a resilience that is essential for great accomplishment." (Dweck, 2015)

I have had the opportunity to work in many different educational environments. My employment history provided me with experiences in public safety, the business world, and managing a large volunteer organization. With all of those experiences, the most difficult challenge is to work with people that possess a fixed or regressive mindset.

The toughest employee, teacher, student, coach, or player, to work with is the one that believes "I am who I am. I'm not going to change, and I've always done it this way." The person with this attitude is the most exhausting

That describes the teacher that uses the same lesson plan every year or the teacher who is reading off yellowing hand-written paper, the 'old ball coach' that won't pass the football because there are three outcomes from a pass, and two of them are bad. NFL Hall of Fame quarterback Brett Favre didn't get many college scholarship opportunities because his high school coach, his dad, didn't believe in throwing the ball. Favre had a cannon!

A person with a fixed mindset avoids challenging situations. They would prefer keeping the status quo rather than taking on a new adventure or a new opportunity. A person with a fixed mindset does not take criticism well and does not like being corrected. If they don't see a direct and immediate benefit to doing something they will not put in the effort.

And finally, fixed mindset individuals are threatened by the success of others. This is a coach that doesn't support the other programs or celebrate the success of a colleague. It is the boss who fails to recognize when an employee has some success or is recognized by others for the work they are doing. Coaches that you recognize as autocratic generally fall into a fixed mindset mentality.

As you would guess, having a growth mindset is the complete opposite of what we just described. With a growth mindset, you have a desire to learn and improve. You can develop your intelligence; you can work your brain like you do your biceps. The growth mindset individual will take on new challenges and is curious about new techniques or tactics in their sport. These are the coaches that push the game to new levels because they are not afraid to try something new.

Inherently people do not like criticism. However, people that embrace a growth mindset look at criticism as a form of feedback. A growth mindset allows you to reflect on the criticism or negative (constructive) feedback as an opportunity for learning. When your player makes a mistake on the field, do you yell and scream at them, or do you look at it as a teachable moment? Do you look at mistakes as an opportunity for growth?

Celebrating the success of others and using that success as inspiration is another example of having a growth mindset. I am an avid reader of coaching books. I want to learn how a coach built their legacy. I am curious to learn how a coach maintains success over a long period of time. When I search for coaching books, I am looking for the coaches that write about leadership and developing the player. There are many books about techniques and strategies. There are biographies, or stories about a successful season. I want the stories about how a coach built a program of character and sustained success. Those are the things that are important to me.

How do we get our players to develop a growth mindset? We have to question them, and we have to guide them. It is time for practice. You set up a drill and you have the players get to work. After a period of observation, you bring the players in and talk about the drill. Many coaches explain the drill, do it for a little while, and then move on to the next drill. To push your players to develop a growth mindset, ask them questions during your training. Provide them problems they need to solve within their game.

Instead of just moving on, assemble the team together and ask them why, "we the team," are doing this particular drill. It would be quicker to tell them. Allowing the team time to examine the reason why in their own minds stimulates growth and learning. Once the "why" is answered, send them back out to try it again. You will see the intensity pick up, the purpose has been identified, and growth happens.

When you take practice time and put players in a game situation, maybe it's a 4th and 2 at the goal line, or an in-bound pass in a tie game with five seconds on the clock in basketball. Then allow the players to come up with ideas of what to do in that situation. Allow time for the players to practice their ideas. Maybe they work, maybe they don't, but the players now become more aware of why they do the things you have instructed. It creates a greater buy-in and will lead to greater success.

If you haven't embraced growth mindset, it is time to stretch yourself and take the risk! Try taking a coaching course, or read about something you haven't thought about. Maybe yoga would be a good addition to your training? I remember in high school our basketball coach did not believe in weightlifting for his players because he said it would affect the player's shooting. Just look at a college or NBA player today. Those players have certainly found the benefits of a weight room.

You are reading this book, so obviously you have a growth mindset. Think of more ways to not only challenge yourself but your team as well.

CHAPTER 7
Athletics Build Character

The Misconception: We are coaching beyond the game; we do not want to lose a season's worth of growth just for a "W".

We talked about coaching styles earlier and how the early days of organized high school athletics were preparing young men for war. It took until 1972 for us to see the value in sports for girls. Title IX changed that landscape. The early belief was that not only did organized athletics train our boys to be fit and strong, but it taught them to follow orders without question. The belief was that coaches were building character when in reality they were training soldiers. Character and blind obedience are entirely different things.

It was also a time where one parent, usually the father, worked and one parent, usually the mother, was always home. Children were taught respect, manners, and character from their parents and grandparents. By the time these young people started playing sports, their character values were already in place. It was because of the character traits their parents instilled in them that they were obedient and listened without question to the coaches before them.

Fast forward to the world today, our children are in a totally different place. The family unit no longer functions like it did one-hundred years ago. The child has more time alone, more technology available, and often both parents are employed full-time. There may only be one parent in the household or they may go back and forth between parents. Who is teaching the child to be polite, to be respectful, to say please and thank you? Many of the character lessons formally taught at home are falling on teachers and coaches.

In the late winter of 2019 and spring of 2020, a pandemic developed that affected the lives of everyone on the planet. Many people started to work from home, and schools were closed down, causing children to be at home. The family unit was forced to be together. For many families, it became a time to reconnect and become closer. Parents started to appreciate and recognize the work that teachers and coaches do to help in the development of their children. Time will tell if this will help strengthen and reinforce our character values.

If you are a transformational coach, character education is already part of your coaching style and an important piece of your team's development. If character lessons and teaching those values are not part of your program, you can't assume that all of your players have been taught what respect means, what it means to take responsibility for their actions, or what the word integrity means. If you want character values to be part of your team's makeup, you have to teach it. Identify the traits that are important to you and teach them.

In our program, we have developed five core values for our team. During the first week of the season, we emphasize one of the values each day. The entire group of players, varsity, junior varsity, and freshmen are all together for the lessons. We spend 10-15 minutes at the start of each of those practices to reinforce the desired behavior, to teach our core character values.

Respect is one of our core values. The first day we gather the group, and we talk about what respect means. Did we show respect for our teammates by making sure we prepared ourselves over the off-season to be ready for today? Did we show respect by recognizing our coaches as we arrive at practice? We talk about respecting our opponents, respecting officials, respecting our parents and our teachers. We talk about when we leave practice today that we respect the facility and leave it better than we found it.

During that first week, our players take home a worksheet, a self-reflection that helps define those values for them. We collect the homework assignments and start to keep a character binder for each of them.

During the first week our team is together for a new season, we cover all five core values. At the end of each week, the coaches decide what additional value we will emphasize the following Monday. We take that value and emphasize it each day. Every time we introduce a new value, the players receives a homework sheet. It is filled out and returned to the coaching staff. We evaluate the work, return it to the player to place in their character binder. Let's take a look at some examples.

When we experienced a disappointing loss and noticed the team was struggling to get past it, the value we choose for the next week was resilience. We took time each day to teach techniques that focus on the "next pass" or the "next play." We pick values that are relevant to a situation we have or will experience as a team. We look for moments in practice where we see reinforcement opportunities to bring attention to the player who positively applies the new lessons. Similar to when we are teaching skills and tactics, look for positive application and praise it.

Another example has to do with your schedule. How does your team look at upcoming opponents? When we look at our schedule, we revisit our value of respect. How do we show respect in the event we are overwhelming an opponent? Coaches know that players can show too much respect to a team and be defeated before they step onto their competitive arena. Players can also lose to an inferior opponent because they did not show enough respect and took the team too lightly. These are discussions that need to part of your pre-game preparations.

The term "trap-game" is often used when a team is looking ahead to the next big game. They see a perceived weaker team on the schedule prior to the big game. The team disrespects the weaker opponent and therefore does not mentally prepare for that contest, often ending with an undesired result.

Your team is starting to have some success. They begin to string together some victories, and their confidence is growing. Now may be a good time to add "quiet-confidence" to the character toolkit. Young men and women need to learn how to carry themselves when they have successes as well as when they experience failures. When respect is a core value and quiet-confidence is added, players recognize the pressure of a big game, and they can use positive self-talk to keep them focused on the task at hand. We can teach them how to "shut out the noise" from the opponent, from the crowd, and from their own head-space.

When your team is blowing-out an opponent, with quiet-confidence, they learn to have fun and play with energy, within the boundaries of respect. Playing the game is not about intimidation and trash-talking, but we often see these behaviors when a team dominates an opponent. When the program is built on character, producing great human-beings is one of the key evaluation measures at the end of the season.

There are many lessons that we can teach our athletes through competition. The transformational coach will recognize moments to provide growth and enhance the players' experience. The end-game is to make them positive members of a larger community.

Let me warn you: When you decide to make character development a part of your program, as the coach, the leader of the program, you will be looked upon to model the characteristics you are teaching. Everyone, not just your players, will be watching you. They want to see if you are really "walking your talk." They listen to not only what you say, but they watch what you do.

When I was the director of a youth organization, not only did my duties include the daily operations of the club, but I trained coaches and coordinated and trained our referees as well. I was in full coach mode during a 10-and-under game when a young referee made a mistake on the field. I yelled across the field, telling this young referee how they had blown the call. The opposing coach called me out during the game.

After the game, I apologized to both the referee and the opposing coach. I realized then that I had to always be cognizant that people were watching me. My behavior, considered normal for any other coach, was not appropriate for me. That incident reminded me that I had to model the behavior I expected from others at all times.

When you teach your players about sportsmanship, you must always model that behavior. There may be an incident in a game that gets under your skin, but your thoughts should be, 'How do I want my players to react?' That should be your guiding question. Coaches need to pick and choose the battles they wish to fight.

We are coaching beyond the game; we do not want to lose a season's worth of growth just for a "W".

As I observe coaches across all levels and across every sport, I pay attention to how they handle officiating, and I watch their team. Coaches who argue every call and blame officials for losses have teams that complain and often lose focus during the game. There are times when a coach has to bring something to the attention of the referees. Coaches realize that a referee will not reverse a call because a coach is complaining. That coach is vocal because they are hoping to bring attention to a behavior, and maybe influence a future call.

As we teach respect, we need to remember to include those men and women officiating our contests. There are too many stories of officials being attacked by parents after the game. Many states are now passing legislation to protect officials and punish spectators, often a parent, for assault. This behavior is unacceptable, but what does that say about all of us when we have to actually pass laws to protect the people that officiate our games?

To start a character-based program, determine what is important to you and your program; those values will be your set of core values. These should be the cornerstone of your program. As your team embraces and starts to embody those values, it is time to add a value of the week. We keep a list of values that we will look at depending on what happened the previous week or what may be ahead for us. Here are a few examples:

Enthusiasm: Doing everything with joy. If we are not having fun, then why are we doing it?

Motivation: Have the players reflect on what motivates them. What is the difference between intrinsic and extrinsic motivation? We try to help them recognize their intrinsic drive.

Compete: Can we compete? This is a good one when the team is going to battle a rival or a program that has been better than ours. How do we compete? Practices are all about competition and overcoming previous results.

Positivity: We try to run a positive program. Asking our players, "what does positivity look like? How do they keep each other positive?

Accountability: What is the player's role in our success, in our setbacks? This is a good value to cover early, especially if players did not prepare themselves properly for the start of the season.

There are many character values that you can pick from. Take a look at the length of your season. If it is fourteen weeks long, then pick fourteen values that you can work on in that time. It can take less than fifteen minutes to do a quick little lesson on the value you want your team to learn. The greatest thing about teaching values is that the impact does not only affect that week or that season. The impact of those lessons will stay with your athletes for a lifetime.

Coaches have the power to not just teach players to "win" on the field, but to teach our young men and women to "win" at life.

CHAPTER 8

The Importance of Relationships

"A common mistake among those who work in sport is spending a disproportionate amount of time on "x's and o's" as compared to time spent learning about people."
–Mike Krzyzewski, Basketball

The key to transformational coaching is not only the ability to build relationships but to understand their value. If coaches spent as much time building relationships with their players as they do working on their playbook, the success of their program would sky-rocket. Coaches are judged on their win total, yet when they put all of the emphasis on winning, they lose focus of the journey. When coaches focus on relationships, the coach will not only see the win total grow, the enjoyment of their job multiplies.

Let's explore some areas where you can start to improve your ability to make building relationships a priority. These tips will not only bring your team more success, they can help improve every area of your life. You can apply these to your job, your significant other, your friends, and your family.

Communication: In the following chapter we will talk about communication in more detail. It is hard to get your message across if you do not talk. It is important that your message gets out. What your plans are for the team? What are the expectations you have for the program? This message must be shared with the players, their parents, the administration, and the community.

Evaluate your delivery system and how you are communicating that to your stakeholders.

Listen: Successful communication is a two-way street. How do you know if your message is being heard? You need to listen to your players, what questions are they asking? If they are asking questions about things you have already shared, maybe you need to change your delivery. Are your players stressed, are they overwhelmed? Ask your players for their input, and listen to what they are telling you. In education, we call that checking for understanding. How often do you check?

When you set team goals for the season, do you tell the players what "their" goals are, or are the players involved in the process? They know a lot about each other, and most of the time the team is aware of their ability. If you listen to the players, you may discover they have lower expectations than what they are capable of. But because you have listened and heard these low expectations, you can plan practices to build them up.

If a coach doesn't know that his team has low self-confidence and yelling and screaming at them for mistakes is their coaching style (autocratic), the team will keep underperforming. Listen to your players! Communication is a two-way street.

Remember the positives: Keep in mind when there are bumps in the road, when a player is making mistakes on or off the field, and you have to talk to them, the player is still a young man or woman or maybe even a child. There may be a reason for their inadequate performance. The player may not have the words to describe why they are a bit off. They may just need a little encouragement to get through a tough time. They may just need someone to believe in them.

Every player on your team brings something positive to the group. Mistakes and missteps are opportunities for learning and growth. It is the job of the coach to provide guidance and help that player to move forward. Every player is a unique individual. Take the time to learn their strengths, and build them up whenever you can.

Don't give up on them: One of my coaches always told our team: if we quit yelling at you, that's when you should worry.

How often do you "give up" on a player? They make too many mistakes, and you start to believe you made a mistake putting them on your squad. You work with them for a while, and then you just quit trying to make them better. Their role on the team is almost non-existent, so you no longer make the effort to help them improve. The player may continue to make attempts to get your attention, and they continue to put in the effort despite the lack of attention you gave them.

A transformational coach will continue to talk to the player. The transformational coach will continue to send a message to that player that they are unique, and their efforts are appreciated. That player's role may be as a substitute or for balancing team chemistry. The role may not include a lot of playing time, yet their place on the team has value. The player needs to be reminded of that, so they stay positive and engaged. They may be training for a more significant playing role for the next season.

The mental health of our students, our players, our employees, are more of a concern than at any time in our history. To be successful in our profession, having a relationship with each player is crucial for success. Family dynamics, break-ups with a significant other, the stress of school, can have an effect on a player's performance. If a player is going through a personal crisis, it can blow-up and affect the practice session. It can alter the chemistry of your team.

Your players need to know that the team is a "safe" place. Coaches do not have to get involved in a player's personal business; however, being aware of an issue can help the coach monitor an issue that could carry over to the team.

Spend time together: Obviously you are going to spend countless hours training together. Take the time to arrange team-bonding experiences away from the game you coach. My teams have gone bowling, played laser-tag, enjoyed mini-golf tournaments, or had paintball adventures.

We have also done community service, allowing us to get out and make a difference as well as work together for a cause. Opportunities off the field/court can help bring the team together on it. There are many ways to enhance the relationship of your team. Be creative.

We are all unique; celebrate your differences: Many of my teams have been comprised of a variety of ethnic backgrounds. Having a team dinner that raises awareness of another culture is a great way to learn about teammates from different backgrounds. A good coach will learn what makes the players unique and celebrate those differences.

Be supportive. Keep each other from criticism and blame. It is easy and ingrained in us to place blame when something doesn't go according to the plan. When your team allows a score, someone made a mistake. A team of character will build up the player that made a mistake and respond positively.

Criticism and blame lead to resentment, causing individual and team performance to decline. The teams that stay supportive when times are tough are the ones that are standing tall at the end of the season.

Disagreements between teammates and between players and coaches will happen. Accept that, and learn from them. These incidents are opportunities to build relationships. Not working through the disagreement can cause a divide that will become detrimental to the team. When these incidents happen, it is important to settle them quickly and continue to move forward. Give each player the opportunity to give their side of the issue, and work for a resolution. When players have the chance to talk and listen to each other, their bond can become stronger.

When it is a coach/player disagreement, there may be no wiggle room. It may be the reluctance of the player to follow the direction of the coach. In this situation the coach should explain the "why" to the player. If the relationship is already strong, chances are the player understands and moves forward. If there is no relationship, and the player cannot adjust, they may have to choose not to be part of the program.

An assistant coach of mine had a hard time adjusting to the direction of our program. We talked about it, and I listened to his arguments. Ultimately, he could not agree to the mission we were about to embark on. The assistant finished the season and moved on. Our relationship remained intact, we just did not agree about the direction of the program, and in this situation, there was no common ground.

If you have a relationship, there is no shame in following a different path.

Keep calm: There are times when a disagreement turns adversarial. As the leader of the program, always keep your cool. This is not an easy ask. When another human is screaming at us, our instinctive reaction is yell back. That situation just gets louder and louder, and nothing good ever comes of it.

If you can remain calm and allow the person to get their issue off their chest, you may be able to diffuse the situation and allow for a conversation to take place. Remember, a large part of building relationships is the ability to listen. Sometimes that means you have to let a person vent.

If you remain calm, the person on the other side of the communication will level out, and you can get to a resolution.

Be present: This means that you must be aware of how your players are responding and behaving. If the team is working hard and giving great effort, show them you recognize it by providing a reward. Maybe you lighten up the conditioning at the end of practice. Maybe you bring popsicles because it has been hot, and their work rate hasn't tapered. Coaches and players, need to always be present in the moment. That is mindfulness. Recognize their efforts and acknowledge them.

Have fun! Many of us did not choose to be a coach because of the financial rewards that we would receive. We chose to do this because we have a passion. If we want to stay sharp and effective, there has to be some reward for us. We have to love it. We should enjoy it. Look for ways to make your training fun and engaging. Change up your practices, plan some drills or games in the training session that are playful. Your players will appreciate it and your relationship will grow.

Flexibility is key: A valuable personal quality of mine is being able to "go with the flow." Crazy things happen all the time. When you model that, you can adapt to any situation, and it reinforces that lesson with your team. When they compete, unexpected things are bound to happen. Your team needs to be flexible and able to respond. As their coach, you can be the role model.

Share power: Control is something that everyone seeks. When you give up control and you share power, the relationship becomes stronger. This is not to say that your team has to be involved in every decision, but find areas where you provide opportunities to share power.

When I take on a program, I look at it as an opportunity to guide a group of individuals. The program has been there before me and will be there after I leave. The players are part of this journey, and they should have a say in what we do. It is "their" team; I am just fortunate to be their leader in this moment. Any success we have is shared, so allow them some input.

The greatest thing about building relationships with your team as you go on your journey together is that those relationships do not end when the players' careers are over. Many of your former players will become like family. They will come back and support the program and many will include you in their life.

Teaching your players these relationship tips will help them in their future careers and future relationships.

CHAPTER 9

The Importance of Communication

"You can have brilliant ideas, but if you can't get them across, your ideas won't get you anywhere."
–Lee Iacocca

When coaches or leaders have difficulties with their team, the root of the problem can almost always be traced to communication. It can be lack of communication on the leader's part or more likely in the coaching world, the recipient is not listening. My advice is to over-communicate. My biggest pet peeve is when people, parents, or community members think a program is "political." In other words, when there's a misconception that some people know more than others. If you are not on the coach's good side, your chances of making the team or playing are diminished. My goal is to be as transparent as possible. The way to do that is to communicate and to communicate by as many methods possible.

In this chapter we will try and discover the many communication practices available. Let's start with the parent meeting. The best way to communicate is to get every stakeholder in front of you. Prior to the beginning of your season, hold a parent meeting. This meeting must be mandatory, requiring both the parents and players to be in attendance.

The goal is for 100% attendance, but no matter how hard you try, there will always be a few that don't make it. Most of the stakeholders will be there. Plan this meeting carefully, and cover all of the things you feel are important. Parents will also pick up on your passion and your concern for their child. You have a chance to show how organized you are and how committed you are to the program. Treat the meeting like a performance. How you are "reviewed" is important. This is your show.

The second best way to give everyone the same message is through an e-mail. I ask for the player's contact information as well as the parents'. When I send a message, I send it to everyone. If a player or parent uses the excuse that they were not informed, I can resend the message with the date it was originally sent. If they miss something important because they didn't read the message, the behavior will change quickly.

In today's environment, there are many computer and phone apps that help a coach with communication. Programs like Teamsnap, Maxpreps, and Remind are apps that parents can sign up for. These tools are designed to make communication easier for the coach to get messages to everyone involved in the program.

It may be effective to find out what social media sites your parents and players frequent and post information on these as well. Do you have a team Twitter, Facebook, or Instagram account? If you have the ability to manage all of them, more power to you. If you find that burdensome, find a parent or assistant that has a desire to keep your social media current. Communicate to your stakeholders which social media form you will use.

In our program we create a newsletter. It is sent out bi-weekly during the season and monthly in the off-season. We send the newsletter to our parents, to our sponsors, to the newspaper, and to our alumni. The newsletter promotes upcoming events, celebrations, and game recaps. The newsletter has pictures, advertisements, and information. We use every means possible to promote our team. I would rather over-communicate than to give a parent an opportunity to say they didn't know what was going on.

There are times when one-on-one communication is effective; however, I will caution coaches to be careful with a one-on-one situation. When dealing with a player or parent concern, the double-team rule should be applied. If I have a "meeting" with a player or parent about a concern, I always have an assistant coach present. Having a conversation with a player about playing time, for example, can be a different message by the time they get home and talk to their parents. When I have a witness to the conversation, there is automatic support if the situation becomes uncomfortable.

There are other communication tools that we need to be aware of: using appropriate tone of voice, articulating, and using humor. When correcting a player, the tone you use can get their attention or cause them to tune you out. If your tone comes across as aggressive and loud, the player thinks you are yelling at them, and they tune you out. Using a conversational tone or lowering your voice causes them to focus more and listen to your message. Be aware of your tone.

Plan out your message, make it clear and concise, articulate. Work on keeping your message short and simple. The simpler the message, the greater chance the message is received and understood.

Use humor. There are many times that coaches, teachers, and leaders take themselves too seriously. Humor makes people feel good and allows your message to come across in a more relaxed way. If you are talking to a hostile crowd, a little humor can get them to lighten up, and it allows them to hear your message.

The final piece of the communication puzzle is to encourage feedback and show gratitude. Listen to what your audience has to say. If your parent meeting is too long or you cover something too much, take that in, and make adjustments for the next one. If they have a lot of questions, write them down, and make sure you put the information in your next presentation.

At the beginning and end of a presentation, remember to thank the audience for their time. Let your audience know that you appreciate the fact that they took the time to listen to what you had to say. Thank them for the opportunity to work with their children.

The reason we communicate is to avoid confusion. Coaches are well aware that their athletes do not always deliver the messages home. It is important to utilize every tool possible to keep everyone in the loop, so no one feels left out.

CHAPTER 10

Conflicts and How We Approach Them

"The quality of our lives depends not on whether or not we have conflicts, but on how we respond to them."
–Thomas Crum

The Parent Coach

If you have been in the youth coaching game for any amount of time, you will have heard horror stories of the parent-coach. These volunteer moms and dads are usually adequate at the recreation level, and it is when they follow their child to the select or travel level that the real issues begin.

I received a call recently from a friend in another state. Their daughter is on a select team for basketball. It is a local team. The girls are in eighth grade and will soon be playing at the high school level. The coach, a father of one of the girls, has been coaching this team for the past five years. The daughter of my friend is a very gifted young athlete, and basketball is not her only sport. The coach's daughter and my friend's daughter were best friends and very competitive young athletes.

In the past two years, leading up to high school, the coach started showing his real agenda. He was always there to promote his daughter. While the two girls were competing and winning together, they shared the basketball, and as a team, they had some outstanding results on the record board. Now, with high school looming, the coach felt a need to bring more attention to his daughter. My friend's daughter was now being instructed not to shoot; she now had a different role than the one that had been so successful to the team. It was apparent from watching some game film that she was losing her passion for the game. This promising young female athlete was losing interest and regressing right before everyone's eyes.

This story is happening on youth sports fields and courts all across the country. Instead of keeping the game fun and allowing this team to take risks, share the ball, and share in each other's joy. An adult's agenda can tear the team apart. The size of this community makes this team the only option available for basketball at this age and this level of play. The season is winding down, and hopefully, once this athlete is in the high school program, the joy of the game will return. She is 13; statistically, she could be one of the 30% that quit before the age of 14. Her trophy case, already packed with basketball, soccer, and volleyball hardware, may be enough. She has been one of the most dominating middle school athletes in some time, yet her glory days could be over. Why? Because one coach, one adult, one dad, had an agenda.

As a father of four, I indeed spent a lot of time coaching my children. I may not have done everything correctly, but I learned a few things that helped me flourish during those seasons.

Treat every child as if they were your son or daughter. If the player was a starter, how would I want my child treated? If the player was a role player, how would I want a coach to address them? As a varsity coach, the expectation was to win, yet I still attempted to get every player into the contest. It doesn't always work out, but my players know if there is an opportunity, I will give it to them.

Communication is vital. All of my players learn their role early in the season. Roles and responsibilities change, but a conversation takes place every time. Whether they step into a more prominent role or they see a reduction, there is no mystery to the player.

When coaching my children, we did not talk about practice and games at home unless they brought it up. I was their dad at home and their coach on the field. Likewise, we did not talk about cleaning their room or curfew times on the practice field.

I have expectations for every player. I made sure that the expectations I have for my children weren't higher than those of the other players. Everyone on the team is held accountable. I have witnessed many coaching dads berate their children during games for making minor mistakes yet brush off mistakes of other kids.

If you are coaching your child, set realistic expectations; set boundaries on what is acceptable to talk about at home. My rule was always that they, my children, had control over our team conversations. We did talk a lot about our teams and our expectations, but it was always on their terms. If we were driving home from a loss, or they did not have a particularly good game, we did not talk about it. It was always their choice if performance was discussed. And always on their terms.

Some sports like basketball and volleyball, with smaller courts and indoor settings, make it seem like you are coaching in a fishbowl. Everything you say is public; spectators and parents are right over your shoulder. If you are a transformational coach, this is not a problem. If you are autocratic or you have an agenda, the setting will reveal your real purpose.

Drugs and Substance Abuse

At some point in your coaching career you will have to deal with a drug-related issue and your athletes. The older the age group that you coach, the more prevalent these instances may become. The question then becomes: how will you approach this growing concern? How will you handle situations when they present themselves?

Some will argue it is not a problem; the behavior has been going on for decades; it is not my problem. According to the National Center for Drug Abuse Statistics (NCDAS), 50% of teens have misused drugs at least once in their lifetime. Alcohol and marijuana are the most popular choices. Alcohol use is at 19.3% for high school students. Marijuana use in 10th graders nationally is at 23.9%, and for 12th graders, it is 35.6%. Those statistics tell us that if we coach at that age level and upwards, there is a strong possibility it will affect the team we coach. So what do we do?

Schools usually have a performance code of conduct. These codes are heavily punitive and do not often show a concern for the athlete. Participation on your team may be what is keeping that player from even greater use. Punishments, while often necessary, without an educational or counseling component will not correct the problem. A transformational coach will want to use that mistake to educate and provide a path for that player's individual growth, while still holding the player accountable for actions that go against team values and ultimately hurt the team's performance.

We are living in an age where mental health issues are talked about more openly than at any other time in our history. We have active shooter drills in our schools, and our children spend more time testing in schools then they spend in a physical education class. School counselors have little time to deal with a student's mental health because the counselors take on tasks administrators did in the past, like scheduling. This pressure to succeed without education about how to relieve stress turns a lot of young people to substance use and abuse for that relief.

As coaches from the youth level on up, we need to educate our children and their parents about the benefits of exercise and being part of a supportive team. At the high school level, during my preseason parent meeting, we address substance use and abuse. It is pointless to tell teenagers not to do it because it is illegal; they do not care. It is useless to say to them not to use drugs because their parents do not want them to because they do not care. I use scientific facts to show the athletes and their parents how drugs and alcohol affect their bodies, their recovery, and their performance.

There are always rumors about players using, even players using before a competition. Vaping has become a more significant issue with teenagers today than people realize. Talk to any teacher or administrator today, and they will tell you what a huge problem this has become. Athletic teams are not immune to this.

Recently, a player of mine came to me and confessed that another player had brought a Dab Pen, a Vape with a Marijuana (THC) load, prior to a game. This player was a key member of our team; he was regretful and realized how it affected his performance and also the performance of our team. He took responsibility for himself. He informed me that other teammates were using as well. His punishment was enforced, but that was not the issue; the issue was how deeply was this affecting the team. Without evidence, how would I bring this up, and how would I educate the team.

An autocratic coach may bring the team together, kick the player that confessed off the team and threaten to remove anyone else participating in the behavior. Some coaches use a scare tactic, hoping that will be the end of the issue. In my experience, the players involved just become more secretive.

We assembled the team and talked about what we can control, our actions and our attitudes. We talked about what was now a team issue. The players were re-educated on how chemicals affect performance. We talked about our core values of respect and responsibility and how personal behaviors affect our standards. Before this meeting, I met with our team captains and discussed how they could take ownership of this issue as a team and work to change the behavior. Once my meeting was over, the captain's took over, and the team came up with a plan. They worked together to hold each other accountable. Accountability to each other was paramount if we hoped to accomplish our goals.

Does this solve the issue? It may or it may not. What it does is get the problem in front of the team. It is an opportunity to re-educate the team on how chemicals can derail our goals and dreams. The group becomes more mindful of each other and how the decisions of one can affect them all. There is consensus building as we work towards something that everyone can live with and agree on. It also provides a leadership opportunity for the captains.

There is no magic answer for substance abuse/use. Our players come to us with issues and concerns that were not discussed two decades ago.

If we as coaches continue to have a growth mindset, we will continue to learn about mental health, the effects of substance use, and any issue that arises that could affect the performance of our team and the development of our athletes.

The Player Who Storms Out of a Practice

It doesn't happen every season, and in fact, it may never happen in a program where transformational coaching is the cornerstone. Even one experience where a player becomes so upset they quit or leave the practice field can be a disruption to your team. When a situation like this develops, there are usually signs leading up to the incident: an altercation, meltdown, whatever term you decide to use to describe the event.

Usually, the problem has been building over some time. In most cases, the athlete does not feel that their talents are being utilized. Through your coaching, you have taught a team-first attitude and have shared the role and responsibility for each player, and this athlete wants more. It may be they feel entitled to more, and they do not believe their voice is heard.

Eventually, they hit their boiling point. It may be a correction the coach made during a drill. It may be how the team was divided for a scrimmage or something the coach said in practice, and all of a sudden, the player snaps. Often, if it gets to this point, it is loud, it is disrespectful, and it is extremely disruptive.

There have been two times in my coaching career this situation has arisen, both earlier in my coaching career. In both cases, the player came into the season with a feeling of entitlement. Each player was upset with their amount of playing time.

When the tantrum or demonstration takes place, I let them leave. It is not a time to engage with the player; it is not a time to get emotional. The coach needs to stay calm, maybe attempt to pull them aside to talk; however, if the player is determined to make a scene, you will not calm them down. It is best to encourage them to go to the locker room as the team continues to practice. You may have to give the team a water break to distance them while you try and encourage the player to leave or calm down. Once the player does leave, do not follow them. If you have an assistant available, the assistant should follow behind them to make sure the problem doesn't escalate in the locker room. With no assistant, you may have to contact an administrator to be in the area until the player leaves.

A follow-up call to the parents would be advisable to make them aware there was an issue at practice. Hopefully, this is an experience you never have to encounter. In both instances where this happened, the problem was more in-depth than something within the team. It is usually brought on by a relationship issue or possibly even substance abuse. Those coaches that get to know their players on more than the sport level may have an idea where the anger comes from. The coach may be able to help the player before the issue becomes a problem they believe they have no control over.

In one of these cases, the player decided to quit. The reason their playing time dropped is because they became interested in other activities, and playing a game was no longer a priority. The second player's issues were much more in-depth, and they got the help they needed allowing them to return to the team.

Take time to get to know your players. Today's athletes have more on their plate than ever before, and having a coach that cares about them helps keep them grounded.

The Entitled Player

Entitlement can happen at any age level. According to the statistics I shared in the youth chapter, only 30% of coaches have any coaching training. This statistic is across all sports. Some of those untrained coaches are parents who fill a need at the club level. Many are coaches for schools and clubs that stepped into a role for extra money or because they felt a calling to coach. They are inexperienced and haven't had the opportunity to take any sport-specific coaching courses.

When an inexperienced coach has the opportunity to guide a gifted child, they may not be prepared. Coaches don't always know that the athlete needs more challenging tasks to keep them on a path of growth. Just like the gifted student in the classroom, the teacher often uses them to "help" teach the other students who aren't picking it up as fast.

Coaches tend to do the same thing, and the gifted player is asked to help their teammates improve. The talented athlete is not progressing because they are asked to help the coach. The player also isn't challenged when the team does physically taxing drills. Over time, that gifted player moves up through the club without being held accountable because of the ability they have.

The player eventually is on a team with a knowledgeable coach. A coach with high expectations for every player. A coach that has dealt with this attitude before and treats the player like everyone else. In most cases, the athlete responds quickly, and the player enjoys being coached. Players will always slack off if coaches allow them to.

So how do you handle this player immediately? As a coach, you establish your expectations, and the player may think this doesn't apply to them. I have a no swearing rule in my practices. When I took over a new team, I covered many practice rules: No jewelry, no phones, practice shirt on, no swearing, and maybe a few more. I had already been told who my "elite" players were, so I made sure the first player I called out for breaking one of these practice agreements was one of these elite players.

I heard an inappropriate word, and the penalty was handed down. When someone swears, the entire team stops what we are doing, and everyone does ten push-ups. The person who let the inappropriate word slip does ten extra push-ups. The first time this happens, the violator almost always protests, but I don't back down. The rule is the rule. This puts the entire team on notice. It may take a lot of push-ups, but eventually the mouth is cleaned up. It is easy to hold the players on the bottom of the roster accountable. Using the best players as the first test subjects show your players that everyone will be responsible for the same standard.

As coaches, teachers, or business leaders, we often overuse the term entitlement. According to the Oxford Dictionary: Entitlement is the belief that one is inherently deserving of privileges or special treatment. The term we may want to start using is "operant conditioning", a method of learning through rewards and punishments for behavior. Through operant conditioning, an individual makes an association between a particular behavior and consequences (Skinner 1938).

To understand operant conditioning as a coach, you need to be aware of the background of your athlete. When your rules or standards have a playing time penalty attached, be prepared to hold your best player accountable, even when you are playing in your toughest games. Once you give in and let a player off the hook, your rule is no longer useful.

"If you want to motivate development, praise effort, not talent. If you want to keep someone from improving, praise the talent."
–Unknown

On the Hot Seat!

In 2018, a long-time high school basketball coach (18 seasons) was in a bar after a game and confronted by a group of parents. This was a coach who took his team to the state semifinals in 2011, had a career record of 207-197, playing in one of the best large school conferences in the state of Wisconsin. Two days after the confrontation, the coach resigned.

The parent's complaints were many: The coach was too hard on his players, they questioned his tactics, the team play was embarrassing, and he yelled at the kids too much.

When the newspaper article came out, there were coaches and players alike that commented about his passion for kids and his caring personality. So what went wrong? Quite simply, the team was losing. This coach had two personalities, his "coaching" personality, and his "teaching" personality. In practice, in games, and on the court, he would've been identified as an autocratic coach. He was very demanding, expecting a lot of his players, and used yelling and screaming as his communication tool.

When he was away from basketball, he was caring, a positive teacher and his passion for education and youth was without question. When the team is winning, parents will praise aggressive coaching behavior because they often relate power and dominance with character building. As we discussed earlier, historically, we expected high school sports to prepare our young men for war or for jobs that required obedience and unquestioning loyalty. Many fathers and grandfathers played high school sports where that style was accepted and the norm.

When the winning stops or the talent pool becomes shallow, the coach's behavior becomes louder than the scoreboard. Parents start to defend their child as they see the anger, the frustration, or the emotion that is almost always just under the surface of the yelling and screaming.

Like many autocratic coaches, the parents of the players are not their concern. The coach is there to mold the team, and it is not in their job description to deal with the parents. In this situation, if the coach would have engaged the parents and communicated more effectively with them, possibly providing avenues for them to feel part of the experience, it may have saved his job, or his desire to continue. This example leads to the next topic.

Going "Out" in the Community

In my early days of coaching, my wife and I were never out in the community. As a teacher, a coach, and a father of four boys, we never had the time or the money. I was under the belief that being seen in a bar, pub, or tavern, was not a good practice. Then I got hired as a junior varsity/ assistant football coach at a small school where the football program was the most important thing in that community. It was an expectation, not an option, that the football staff show up at the local tavern after the game. Community members and parents were there to discuss the game and meet the coaches. It was not a comfortable setting for me, but one that I was expected to be part of. I would show up, have my soda, talk to a few people, and then quietly excuse myself. I had diapers to change.

Many communities may have traditions or expectations that are part of the job. If an appearance is expected, the recommendation is to keep it brief and leave before a situation could develop. While these gatherings can be fun when times are good, there will be a time when the team is struggling, and the tide turns on you. Keeping your obligations brief and responsible will help you avoid that uncomfortable confrontation.

It comes down to setting boundaries. In the next chapter, we will talk about parents and how you get them on your side, how to establish boundaries, and how to help keep those relationships positive.

Lack of Support

I was watching the local news, and the big story had to do with three varsity football coaches stepping down from coaching after only three years at the helm — three different coaches, three different schools, one common theme, lack of support. As the coaches were interviewed, they said a lack of funding for what they needed was a big concern, but the biggest complaint was lack of support from the administration.

When coaches, teachers, or employees complain about a lack of support, it could mean many things. A football coach asking for a brand new turf field to compete in their conference complains about lack of support. When the administration says no, because of funding, yet the coach persists putting their needs ahead of every other sport, that does not make a compelling argument.

If you do not get something you want, it may have more to do with available funds, other program needs, or lack of research. A strong relationship with the athletic director or administrator will keep the request on the queue, but an understanding of the reality of the request would be more realistic. Some requests are wants and not needs. That is not a lack of support; it is just reality.

Recently a coach stepped away from his girls' varsity soccer team mid-season. Once again, the reason was lack of support. The coach had been in the program as a junior varsity coach for a few years, the varsity position opened up, and he was excited as he took the reins of a varsity program that had hovered around .500 for the past five seasons. He was going to be the change.

He brought in a character-based agenda and started to build relationships. Culture change does not happen overnight, and while the coach was introducing his vision, the results (wins), were not materializing. Parents, at times, can be impatient, and before you know it, a complaint flowed to the athletic director's desk. Someone said that the girl's new varsity coach was calling the girls "bitches." The coach denied the allegations, he had his players reinforce his story to administration, but the complaint took root. The coach did not feel he had the support to fight it, and he didn't want to get fired and jeopardize future opportunities, so he stepped away.

The coach was upset with his athletic administrator because at no time in the previous two months, the start of his first season, did the athletic director watch a practice or attend a game. The athletic director listened to others instead of defending the coach. That school, more than likely, lost a dedicated and responsible coach because of a complaint made by an influential parent. So how do you, as a new or veteran coach, avoid a similar issue?

The first thing the coach should've done, before even accepting the coaching position, would've been to lay out his character-based plan for the school's soccer program. The coach should have scheduled a prior conversation with the administration to talk about how he was going to impact the mediocre mentality of the program. He should have laid out his plan for how he was going to affect that change. The idea, as well as his expectations, could've been printed out and left for the athletic director. Also, emphasizing that improper language would not be tolerated in his program.

The next step before the season began would be to set the expectations with the parents and players. The parents would be part of the educational process to change this culture, understanding that actual change can happen quickly but does not happen overnight. A process would be laid out and followed.

These two steps may have been able to keep a coach in a sport he was passionate about. First, he would have begun a strong relationship with his administrator. The administrator would have questioned the complaint because he/she knew inappropriate language was not allowed in this program. Secondly, if their relationship had been based on mutual trust and understanding, the administrator would have channeled that initial complaint back to the coach. The parent with the claim should know to address this concern with the coach first. It would've allowed the coach to further educate a parent on what it was the program was trying to accomplish.

Finally, the coach, realizing that his administrator had yet to attend a practice session or a contest, should have made attempts to welcome the AD to his sideline. The lack of support and communication certainly is not just a problem for this coach, and there is probably a more significant issue with the entire athletic program. More coaches are probably in jeopardy because the person in charge has no connection to those that work for them.

We could continue to share coaching horror stories, but avoiding conflict is pretty simple. Treat everyone in your program as a stakeholder. Use all of your tools of communication to share your message and your vision. Put yourself in that state of mindfulness. What would you want if you were on the other side?

CHAPTER 11

What Parents Want and How to Win Them Over

"We all need a cheering committee and parents are a child's most important fans!"
–Vivian Kirkfield

I know many coaches that are afraid to deal with parents. Many coaches view parents as problems, and they do not realize that if you agree to coach their kids you also need to be prepared to coach the parent. Once you take the time to understand what parents really want, you can be much more effective not only in how you communicate with parents but also in your dealings with them. My approach to the parental "problem" is simple. Parents have been sacrificing time and money to provide the best experiences for their children. If the child likes a sport or activity, parents spare no expense in trying to provide opportunities to help them succeed. By the time the child is older and their babies grow into young adults, the parent receives less feedback from the child. Parents want to feel part of the experience that they made all the sacrifices for.

Many coaches provide information to their athletes assuming those athletes are relaying that information to their parents. The coach that doesn't also include the parent, does not know if the information made it home. How many times have you collected equipment at the end of the season, and in the equipment bag is every handout you sent to the parent? No wonder that parent was never at the events you scheduled.

There are many articles on the different types of parents, and I will touch on a few, but first here are some of the things that parents want.

They want to know their child is treated fairly.

You can give your playing time speeches and talk to your team about roles and responsibilities, you may even have parent meetings where you explain all of that. When parents see you following through on your message, when parents see you hold the star player accountable for the guidelines you have set, they can support you even when their child is the last one off the bench. When you build a relationship with every player, that bench player communicates positively about you when they talk to their parents.

They want to know you care about their child.

At my end of the season banquets I tell a story about every player. Each player receives a goofy award that signifies something embarrassing or comical they may have done during the season. When parents see you give attention to every player on the roster, not just the stars, they can see that you care about your team and that you care about THEIR child. They want their child to play for you.

They want to feel part of the experience.

As I stated in the beginning, the child's path to a spot on a high school age team has been a family journey. Family vacations are often centered around youth sporting events. Parents are now watching a team where they are truly just the by-standers. They may feel separated from their child's experience and alone. It is important to provide opportunities for involvement so they continue to feel part of the experience.

As a child grows and moves on to higher level teams, parents may start to feel more and more disconnected. At one time, all of the teammates were from the same community, the parents were all friends, and the players all attended the same school. As the child advances in development, team placements may change, and parents have less control. Your player is still their child and the opportunity for parents to watch them play a game may be coming to an end.

Only 1 in 14 kids, 7%, go on to play a college varsity sport. Once high school is over, watching a child play in a competitive environment is over. Having a child be part of a team is no longer a family activity. When coaches realize that parents have been supporting a child for 18 years, they have been sacrificing since the child could pick up a ball, then it is easier to look for ways to get them involved.

Always be mindful of what a parent is struggling with. If it is their first child, while it may be traumatic, they still have other children that may follow in the sport. If it is their last child, it can be a sobering experience. The realization hits that an important part of their life is coming to an end. Allow parents to plan the post-season banquet, and allow them to do special things for the team. Cherish them, and allow them to be part of the program.

They want good communication.

There is a correlation between the age of the player and the amount of communication the player has with their parents. A coach that wants to have not just a good relationship but a great relationship with parents, will utilize every means possible to communicate and stay transparent.

Create an email list that includes parents and players, and utilize it often. Create a weekly newsletter during the season, and send it out monthly during the off season. Keep your sport relevant and on the minds of the parents and players throughout the entire year. Celebrate team success, academic success, and community service opportunities. The more the parents know, the better they will feel about you and about the program.

Be Transparent

The biggest complaint heard by parents has to do with politics. How often do you hear, "This club is so political", "The coach only plays his favorites", or "If you volunteer your time or you make a large donation your kid will play".

I could certainly go on. These comments happen when the communication is poor and parents feel like they are out of the loop. When you utilize good communication tools, when your message is put out on many different forums, it is hard for a parent to make statements like those listed above.

Take a little time to reflect on your program. How would you rate yourself on your level of communication? How would you rate yourself on getting your parents to feel part of the program? What are things you could do to improve that area of your coaching?

They want you to fix their child.

There are some parents that are hoping that you "fix" their child. Sometimes parents lose control of their teenage child. For whatever reason, they have allowed their child freedoms before they were ready, and the child has made poor decisions that you, as the coach, may not even be aware of. There are many family dynamics, single parents, parents who are divorced and share custody, or parents that hold down multiple jobs and are not home when the child needs some guidance. Unless the athlete has a relationship with you and shares that information, a coach is not aware of the struggles that may be going on in a family.

The parents don't share this with the coach, but you are an authority figure, and they are hoping you can influence the child's behavior. If you teach character values in your program, you may actually have an effect. The point here is: fixing their child may be a parental expectation you are not even aware of, and WAY above your paygrade.

The statistics are scary! According to Syracuse.com, a news source out of New York, 58% of high school coaches have considered quitting because of parental issues. 82% of the coaches surveyed, Sept. 2016, believe that dealing with parents has become worse since they entered the profession. Eighty-seven percent of the coaches said that playing time complaints were a serious issue, and 67% of the coaches said that unsportsmanlike conduct of parents was out of control. Sixty percent of coaches state that they have had to personally deal with an unruly parent.

There was a time when I was considering a move to the college coaching ranks. Before embarking on this endeavor, I sought the advice of a local collegiate coach. He told me he could never coach high school and deal with the parents. One of his favorite things about coaching at the collegiate level was the lack of parental interaction.

Young people who are considering coaching have to be questioning that decision when all they hear are horror stories about parental behavior. There are numerous articles or news reports of bad parent behavior, and it seems to be getting worse. We have to look for the positive parental behaviors and celebrate them. Unfortunately, the bad behavior sells. Before we start to fix the problem, let's examine the different types of parents.

My Child Is Special – Prince/Princess

A coaching colleague of mine was coaching a high school girls team. He coaches in a very affluent area. Many members of his team had attended high-level camps and were always treated to the best there was to offer. The parents were demanding and often critical of the smallest things. The team was very successful, yet they still found fault with things that the team was doing. There was a core group of moms on the team that traveled to games in their white Escalades. They often followed each other and arrived at the same time to the event. He referred to these moms as the "blond mafia".

The girls were treated like princesses; this is a perfect example where expectations need to be stated clearly. Every player regardless of talent or influence needs to be held to the same standard. Parents want to know that their child will be treated fairly.

Helicopter Parent

This parent, also referred to as the "hover" parent, is always around. They are around before practice, after practice, and they want to hear your assessment after games. They can be critical, but often they just want to feel connected and close to the team. They may be keeping an eye on their child and evaluating their child's performance to those around them. It would be a good idea to find this parent a job or responsibility to keep them occupied. As soon as something happens that they don't approve of, they can become a thorn in your side. Keep them busy!

M.I.A – Missing in Action Parent (Dry Cleaner Parent)

The player who has this parent usually has no support system at home. The parent likes that they are busy and involved but doesn't really care about the team or how the child is performing. This player will need a lot of positive reinforcement and a little extra attention.

If you need parents to help with the program or fundraise, they will not be around. The player may feel guilty because everyone else's parents do a lot for the team, but their parent is never around. As the coach you may also have to make sure this athlete has a ride to and from practice because the parent will always be late. It may be necessary to find another parent who will help or "adopt" this player during the season.

Tiger Mom

We have all experienced this parent. They drive their child and set high, sometimes unrealistic expectations. This athlete could be extremely high strung and stressed. Not only are there high expectations for performance on your team, but the same is expected for their academics.

This player could be prone to outbreaks in practice or games when they don't feel they are performing to a parental expectation. This parent could be in the stands, and one word could throw the child off their game.

There was a female athlete that had played for our soccer club. Her father was a "tiger mom" and set high expectations for her. She was very talented and was in the state's Olympic Development Program. She went on to play for a different high school than the one I coached at, and our teams met in the semi-final of a weekend tournament.

It was a close game at the beginning, and her team was awarded a free-kick from thirty yards out. She made an unbelievable shot on the goal - hit the corner of the cross bar - but missed the shot. Her father screamed his disappointment from the stands so loud you could hear it all over the athletic complex. At this point the game was over. We went on to score four goals and win the game. Every time this young lady took a shot or had another free-kick it wasn't even close to the goal.

His comment shut her down better than we were able to. If the parent goes to this extreme, the coach has to address the issue. It is an uncomfortable conversation, but the parent needs to recognize the "one-voice" philosophy. There can only be one-voice while the team is playing. The only one the player should listen to or even hear is that of the head coach. This kind of parent is common, and many coaches don't feel confident enough to confront the problem. Either confront that parent or live with the losses.

Lawn Mower Parent

This is the newest label for a parent in today's coaching world. This term was given to the latest epidemic where parents are cutting down any barriers a child will have to face to participate on a team. If there is a requirement that the athlete needs to complete, the parent will do it for them if it is possible. An example would be if a player is required to find a sponsor for the program. The parent, instead of helping the athlete prepare and approach someone, goes out and does it themselves.

If this parent doesn't approve of what you are doing in the program, they bypass the conversation with the coach and plow right through to the athletic director, principal, or president of the club. A strong chain of command is needed to keep the lawn mower parked.

Remember the college coach I spoke about? This type of parent has made their way into the college realm and collegiate coaches are now experiencing the lawnmower parent.

The Coach Parent

This parent sits in the stands and becomes a problem because they express strong opinions, usually negative. This parent has coached these players at some other time in their development. Other parents surround this parent because they were the "youth" coach. This parent makes comments like, "Our team was undefeated during our U12 season. Why is this team not winning at the varsity level? Well let me tell you why!"

This parent, if not confronted, will end up leading a charge that may put a coach's position in jeopardy. The former coach of your players will tell those around them that they have all the answers. They know what works because it worked when the kids were younger. Often the other parents will listen because of a past relationship. On the flip side, this parent may be a loud mouth that has overstayed their welcome and be a nuisance to those around them. Whatever the case may be, if there is no other parent that takes an opportunity to settle them down, that delightful task may fall on your shoulders.

This parent may just be the one that is constantly coaching their child after every game, prior to every game, and from the sidelines. This parent may speak badly of your game decisions at home, and those conversations may make it into your practices. The player may question your decisions because what you are saying is not the same as the parent.

Before this behavior starts to affect a player's performance, it is time to have a conversation with the parent. This is a conversation the should be scheduled with an administrator. The meeting is an opportunity to re-educate the parent about expectations and the values important to the team.

The Negative Parent

This parent never has anything good to say about the coach, the program, the referees or the other players on the team. They are extremely annoying, but sometimes bad seeds with a little fertilizer will grow.

I found that asking a parent to be the enforcer in the stands works well. I pick out the mom who has a gregarious personality and a mom that everyone seems to enjoy being around. I arm her with a bag of suckers, and when someone is negative or screaming at the referees, she quietly slips them a lollypop. We discuss the lollypop at our preseason meeting, and it is the team's way of telling someone to simply enjoy the game.

This has been very effective throughout the years.

I'm "Living Through My Child" Parent

Similar to the tiger parent, this parent often doesn't know when they should shut their mouth. Coaches who cover the one-voice message at their parent meetings set the standard for parent behavior on the sidelines. I learned to share the following at my parent meetings. There are only four jobs when it comes to our team: 1 Coach; 2 Player; 3 Official; 4 Spectator.

I am the coach, so that job is taken, at least for this year. Therefore, I am the only one that gets to make coaching decisions and give directions. The player. That is your child. Besides, you are too slow, and your skill has deteriorated. The third is the official, and while you may be certified and know all the rules, the people out there were hired for this contest, so we will let them do their jobs. Finally, the spectator. That is you. Enjoy the game, watch your child play and be part of the team. Cheer for every member of our team, and always practice good sportsmanship.

If you have coached or are currently coaching, you have more than likely experienced all of these parents at one time or another. Maybe you had a different name for them, but you recognize the behavior and have successfully or unsuccessfully dealt with them. It will help save your career and your sanity if you come up with a plan to handle these parental types before you have an issue.

CHAPTER 12
Controlling the Narrative

"Hope for the best, but prepare for the worst."
-English proverb

You signed up to coach, you love the game, you want to share your knowledge and your passion. Now that you are in the profession, regardless of the age-level you are coaching, you are beginning to realize that coaching is more than just Xs and Os. You are finding out you have to be a counselor, a parent, possibly even a member of the clergy. You are not only answering to your players, but their parents, your administrators, the community, and your fan base.

Little did you know when you signed up that you would be your own public relations department. You are most likely not equipped or educated to be a promoter. You signed up to coach. In this chapter you will learn the importance of controlling the narrative and to be your own best promoter.

Let's examine four areas you can focus on as you start to become your own PR department. The very first thing you want to do is to define your values. What values will define your program? We are not talking about the offenses and defenses you plan to implement; we are talking about a standard of behavior

A program with core values and a program that lives those values is able to ward off many issues that may be the demise of other programs. When the coach sets expectations and holds all stakeholders accountable to those expectations, the narrative begins to take root. Let's begin with the preseason parent meeting. The coach describes and implements the chain of command. It is made clear to all parties the process for handling grievances. An incident occurs, a parent decides to go directly to the coach to complain or campaign for their child. When the coach responds by telling the parent that the chain of command requires a conversation with the player first, it adds more strength to the process.

If the coach gives in and has a conversation with the parent, violating their own rule that the coach/player conversation is the first step, the chain has now weakened. The message has been sent to everyone that your chain of command was only a suggestion. This lapse in judgement will tell everyone that they can now go directly to the coach. This leads to many unwanted discussions with parents when the issue probably could've been handled with a player/coach conversation.

When standards are set and modeled, everything that happens both positive and negative can be directly related to the standard. An example for this may be athletic paperwork. Your administration requires a number of signature forms and permission documents before a player can compete. You put these requirements out to your team, and it is then the responsibility of the player to complete the required task. When the player doesn't follow through and misses the activity, that can be a lesson about responsibility.

Consistency will help you build trust and good will. When every player is treated the same, people around the program notice. When a disgruntled parent is complaining in the stands, others will continue to support you and your program because they know what you stand for.

The second thing that will help with setting the narrative is to follow the 3 Ps: Plan, Prepare, and Practice. Make a plan for the season. Plan for every travel event, any team building event, home game preparation, away game needs, player expectations, and any other event your team will take part in. Think about all possible scenarios that may come up during the season: a parent complaint about playing time, a devastating injury, or a player ejection, just to name a few.

When these situations arise, do you have a plan? Do you have an idea of how you would respond? When you see a coach that encounters a problem with his team, write it down. What if that happened to your team? Plan for an event that hasn't happened yet. Always be prepared!

Maybe something happened that you were not prepared for in the past, and you did not handle it very well. Reflect on that incident and how would you correct that problem if it happened this season. If you have a plan, you can then prepare.

You coach your team. You work on situations that could occur during the course of play. You work tirelessly on making sure your team is prepared for anything your opponents can throw at you. A coach that wants to plan for a long career will need to prepare for circumstances that can happen off the field as well.

The third "P" is practice. Take the time to gather your coaching staff and practice dealing with an irate parent. Practice a scenario where a player comes to you to talk about playing time. What language will you use? How will you massage the player's ego yet keep them positive and working hard for the team? Every possible situation, once identified, can be practiced.

Another thing to remember is that your stakeholders need to be reminded regularly what your message is. Your values need to be displayed, printed on programs, on t-shirts, and talked about often. Ideas like your chain of command, playing time philosophy, and your mission, should be communicated often.

Communicating today is often challenging. Your players are into many different media platforms. Young people do not check email like their parents do. Young people are moving away from Facebook, but their parents and grandparents still utilize that platform.

Our program utilizes Twitter, Facebook, and Instagram for the people that like those outlets. We still use email, and we started publishing a bi-weekly newsletter. We post current happenings and pictures on social media sites, and we share news and upcoming events in the newsletter. Our email list is used for timely delivery of information. We include sponsors, administration, and media in our distribution.

There are also many team apps for phones that are available. At some point you have to decide which of these will serve your purpose the best and stick with them. All of this is so that you are able to keep your message in front of your stakeholders.

Public relations departments work very hard pushing a positive message out to their customer base. A PR department really earns their money when there is a crisis. Most coaches do not have the luxury of a PR department or a sports information department, so they not only coach but handle public relations as well. When there is a crisis, being able to communicate your message early and often helps keep the program moving forward.

Coaches who share information and make all their materials available have a better chance of surviving a negative situation in the program. Let's look at a possible problem that could derail everything you have worked for.

You have a standard, maybe a code of conduct policy that your players have to sign and agree to follow. You have a player that is showing signs of using a substance that violates that code. You have suspicions, maybe even some of the teammates have voiced their concerns as well. As always, you have many different ways to handle the situation. Many will just ignore the situation. There is no proof, yet you have been coaching long enough and know your instincts are correct.

Ignoring the issue, the elephant in the room, sends a message to your team. You talk about respect and responsibility yet you avoid taking the responsibility to help this player make better decisions. When you avoid the issue your players now realize that maybe you don't really care about them, you just want to win. Your message loses credibility.

Another option: hold a team meeting and talk to the entire team about behaviors that can be detrimental to the team. You believe you are addressing the issue, and you and your team can move on. The problem with this method is that the only players that are listening to you are the ones making the right choices anyway. The players participating in questionable behavior are ignoring you.

You can pull the player aside, have a conversation, maybe tell the player that if you hear anything more, they are done and off the team. This may help, but what happens when they do mess up? You both know it has been going on for quite some time, but the parents have no idea. You remove the player, and now the parents are complaining to you, the administration, and the community about how you singled out their child and accused them of something you had no proof of; now your program is in a crisis.

My recommendation is to pull the player aside, and with another adult, talk to them about the concern. Emphasize the values of your team and why they are important. Make sure the player knows you are there to help them be a better athlete but more importantly a better person. If you are a transformational coach, you have already been building a relationship with the athlete, and the difficult conversation will be easier.

I would then go an extra step and communicate with the parent. Explain your concerns, your conversation, your willingness to help, but make it clear the player's spot on the team could be in jeopardy. If that situation develops down the road, by having that conversation with the parent, you will probably avoid a crisis if the player has to be removed from the team.

Many years ago I had an underclassman that possessed talent we had not seen in our program. He had long flaming red hair and was easy to identify. During the season he started turning his hair into fiery red dreadlocks. During the off-season rumors were circulating about possible drug use. His grades were dropping, and his teachers were starting to talk to me about his behaviors. He was turning assignments in to his teachers with pot leaf drawings all over them.

It wasn't long before he was picked up for underage drinking. His parents were a little concerned, but they were not too worried; drinking was typical teenage behavior. I talked to him a few times during the winter about his choices, but he always said everything was fine. Then in the spring he shaved his head, removing the dreadlocks, but he had shaved "420" into his buzz cut.

It was early spring; it was time to bring the parents in and have a conversation. The parents had no idea that "420" was a number associated with the use of marijuana. The issue was bigger than soccer, and with the parent's involvement, the player started to get some help. As coaches, we are often the first to recognize when a player is starting to drift away. It is part of our position to share that information with the player's parents.

Good communication is a tool that most coaches do not do enough of. You need to be your own public relations department. Do you have the time to also be your own PR director? Probably not. The benefits of keeping all of your stakeholders informed will make it worth the time and help eliminate many of the pitfalls your colleagues are having.

CHAPTER 13

What Will Be Your Legacy?

"If you're going to live, leave a legacy.
Make a mark on the world that can't be erased."
–Maya Angelou

Stephen Covey says, "Begin with the end in mind."

How many of us get into coaching and think about the end? When we look at the transformational/mindfulness brain, we discussed the different pathways of entrance into the coaching profession. When reflecting back on your coaching beginnings, how many thought about your future in the profession? The same could be said when you took your first job with a company: did you ever think you would be in a position of leadership? When you accepted that middle school coaching position, did you believe that someday you would be the face of the high school program?

We knew we wanted to coach, but did we have a plan for our future? Many young coaches are trying to make their mark; winning is the only thing they are thinking about. Most coaches think about their legacy closer to the end of their careers than the beginning.

I would challenge you to answer the following questions when thinking about leadership/coaching.

What do you want? Is it fame? Is it glory? Are you in pursuit of a championship? Is it the relationships?

Know where you want to go. Why do you want this position?

Is your desire for the greater good? Or are you looking for the title? The perks?

I listened to a university president talk about how he ended up in his role. He was passionate about higher education. He was in tune with the needs of the students. His mission was to reframe some of the undergraduate degrees to truly represent what the clientele was looking for. His purpose was and continues to be for the greater good.

Some pursue a position of this importance because the presidency includes use of the university's private jet and the presidential box at the football and basketball games. Those without a higher purpose generally struggle to hold the position for very long because they do not have a purpose. Their desire was for the position, the title, not for the greater good.

When I first picked up a football, I was going to play in the NFL. At six-years-old, nothing was going to stop me! All through high school, as a bruising 5'7", 145-lb running back, I was still on that path. No one could tell me differently. I was going to make it! Reality hit during my first semester of college. I was hit so hard in practice that I spent the next few months in the training room. So much for being ready for the NFL.

I knew I wanted to teach and coach, and my first head coaching opportunity came at the middle school level. It was at this level that coaching became meaningful. Our school philosophy was about development and exploration. As a teaching and coaching staff, we were all on the same page. Our mission was to inspire young boys and girls to pursue their interests and experience new challenges. There were no middle school championships, records were not a focus. Participation and developing a passion for the activity was the priority.

As a coach, I worked with the high school staff and utilized their schemes and terminology, but my role was to develop passion and motivate young people to continue playing. Coaching youth and middle school-age children grounded me and put me on the transformational path. I still did not think about leaving a legacy.

In 1998, I signed my first contract as a varsity boys soccer coach. I still was not thinking long-term. My experiences in those first few years left me with more questions than answers. I did not have a chain of command,

and I did not have a parent guide. Communication with parents was not a priority. I had some success on the field, but I was experiencing parental demands that did not occur at the middle school level. I was not thinking of a legacy. I was thinking about survival.

I started to self-reflect during those first few years. I looked at successful coaches from every sport arena. Having a growth mindset allowed me to challenge myself as a coach. I continue to use growth mindset to improve in every aspect of my life, not just coaching.

It does not matter if this is the first year in the profession or you are nearing the end of your career. How can you influence your legacy? What is the most meaningful message expressed throughout your career? How do you want your players and your community to remember you? Set the narrative, build relationships, celebrate every season, and celebrate every child.

I leave you with a question from Michael V. Martin, President of Florida Gulf Coast University.

"Can I transform a life a little bit today?"

CHAPTER 14
Putting It All Together

"Life can only be understood backwards; but it must be lived forwards."
–Soren Kierkegaard

Now that you have read the information about what a transformational coach looks like, you should have a desire to be more mindful and bring your players or your employees into a state of mindfulness. You realize you can improve your team by applying these concepts. Yet, it's still not clear: "How do I accomplish this?"

Reflection is something that should be done often and with much thought. You plan out each and every practice session, and then you implement the session. What do you do when it's over? Do you put away the equipment and leave? Of course not! You should take a few minutes in the car, in your office, or on a bench and reflect. Asking yourself a few questions:

How did the session go?

What did the team struggle with?

What do we still need to work on?

How can I make this session better?

A coach that is attempting to teach mindfulness to their players will have the team reflect on the session as well. It is an opportunity for immediate feedback. Maybe you are not ready for a team reflection, and a personal reflection is where you want to start. However, allowing your players or employees to offer their feedback opens up communication and buy-in.

My coaching career spans many seasons. My current team is a group of high school age boys, or in this case - young men. I have a new assistant coach who agreed to take on the task as a JV coach, but he also serves as an assistant to our varsity program. His condition, before committing to the position, was that he be provided with mentorship. He is striving to be a more complete coach and challenge himself to become more holistic in his approach.

For me, that means I am taking more time to write up my coaching plans. Things that I take for granted in my own planning I am writing more specifically into the daily plan because I am sharing these plans with a mentee. This mentoring role that I have agreed to has given me the opportunity to refine my coaching sessions and really reflect on what I am trying to do with my team.

My training begins with an active warm-up period that includes skills needed in that day's session. I decided to change things up a little, and I had the team play a tag game. It was explosive, inclusive, and physically taxing. These young adult men had so much fun chasing each other around that they forgot they were actually conditioning. When we, as a team, reflected on the training session prior to leaving that day, they decided they wanted to play more tag games in their warm-ups.

Once the team left and I did my own reflection on our session that day, I learned that our tag game enhanced our training session for the day. It strengthened our team core value and allowed us to simply have fun.

The message here is that personal reflection is the first place to start when embarking on this holistic journey. Ask yourself, what is your coaching style? If you aren't sure, look for a coach in your community or in your sport that you believe is practicing a style you want to emulate. Ask that coach if you can watch some of their training sessions, maybe even ask them to come and watch your sessions. If you are open to constructive feedback, you are ready to move forward on your coaching journey towards mindfulness.

We talked earlier about having a growth mindset. I was asked once how often do you change things up in your coaching? When do you know if you made it? My answer was simple: you don't. When you think you know everything or you think there is no new material to learn, you start falling into a regressive mindset.

My own coaching experience spans over four decades. I am continually reading new coaching books, attending coaching conventions, and learning from my peers. The games we coach are always changing, and we need to stay current. If you are in business, you experience the same things. If you do not stay current with your clientele, the methods of communication, or their changing needs, you fall behind, and you lose.

Another question experienced coaches are asked: how do you know when you have made a difference? Again, you may never fully know the impact of your coaching. Take a moment to reflect on your own playing experience. What do you remember about your youth or high school coaches? If they had a positive influence on your life, have you ever told them? I think I was in my early 40s when I finally sent a letter to my high school football coach thanking him for the impact he had on me. Recently, I was asked to write a letter of recommendation for a player that I coached over a decade ago. I would not be able to do that if we did not have a relationship that has continued well past his playing days.

You have done your self-reflection and realized that there are a lot of changes you would like to make. It will be a difficult task if you try and tackle everything at once. It is time to prioritize and make a plan. This is just like when planning the season, but instead it is a self-improvement plan. What do you feel is the most important area that needs to be addressed? Which ideas can be implemented quickly and which ones need to be developed over time? Are there any areas where you can find some help?

There are two things I think must take place immediately: establishing your core values and your chain of command. I remember when I decided that I needed to have core values for the program I was involved in. At the time, our athletic department did not have anything in place. Every coach was on their own, and there was no guidance from our athletic administration. My staff and I met, I explained the direction I wanted to take the program, and we developed our values.

During the season, we hired a new athletic director, and we had a discussion about the core value program I was putting in place. Our administrator thought we should have a set of core values for our entire athletic program. We had 23 sports, and we both agreed that having consistent values across all of the sport offerings would benefit our students and make our athletic program stronger.

While I continued to teach and model the values we had set for my program, we held meetings with our entire high school coaching staff and came up with character-based values we could all implement and teach across the entire department. The process to communicate the need and educate our coaching staff on the value of such a program took us a year to finalize, develop, and implement. In the beginning of our next school year, we were able to promote a character-based value plan across all sports.

The point here is that while this process took over a year to implement, I was still able to put a value program in place while everyone else caught up. Each year I try and add something different to the way we present the information to the team. For example, one year I gave the team notebooks, and I had them keep a journal during the season. I would give them prompts, and they would have to write a "reflection" with that prompt.

Every two weeks, on Friday, I would collect the journals, read them and make a comment. That has now developed into a thin binder. We pass out a three-ring binder at the beginning of the season. Each day during the first week of practice, we discuss one or our core values. The team then receives a handout to fill in and place in their binder. I still collect them every two weeks. Collecting them and writing comments holds the player more accountable to putting their thoughts down.

At the end of the journal are pages for self-evaluations after each contest. They write what they did well, where they could improve, and something about the opponent should we meet them again. Players are encouraged to write about their concerns as well. Maybe they want to try another position, maybe they are worried about playing time and they want to know what I need to see for that to manifest.

This journal has been a positive tool for enhancing our communication. We also use the journal to pass out set pieces, strategies that we may use in a contest. There are roles and responsibilities of the positions, making the players more aware of not only their job but that of the player next to them. The journal is theirs to keep at the end of the season. It is their playbook and their diary of that time in their life.

This is not an easy task. I would be lying to you if I said everyone does a great job with this. I have found that anything I do with high school age boys is a struggle. They have to be reminded constantly, and there has to be a purpose. It is important that collected material is read and commented on.

Girls, on the other hand are fantastic with this communication tool. Their handwriting is certainly better, but they love expressing themselves. As the coach, you must pay attention to what is written and be sincere in your comments back to them.

This tool can ward off potential problems as well. During one season, a young man commented on how he thought another player was being picked on by some upper-classman. The complaint was early in the season and could lead to a possible bullying, harassment, or hazing situation if not addressed. As a coaching staff, we were able to use our core values to stop something that could have put a black mark on our program. Instead, we were able to provide a learning opportunity and turn a potential negative into a positive.

The questions for many now become: 'When do I know that I have reached the pinnacle? How do I know that I am truly a transformational coach? When have I completed that journey?"

Those questions cannot be answered by anyone but you. Many coaches who base their careers on achievements or milestones may never have been transformational. An autocratic coach may find themselves on top of the mountain with wins and even be recognized in the school or state Hall of Fame, yet never built a relationship with a player. Those coaches believe they were a great coach. They were fortunate to have great athletes, and winning was their measurement stick.

The career of a transformational coach is never complete. Even after retirement or moving on to another coaching situation, the relationships that are built with players will follow. Players will still ask for letters of reference, reach out on social media, send you a card, call you because they are in the area, or invite you to their wedding. Your team becomes an extension of your family; you may not see them for years, and then you connect, and it's as if you never left.

When you have a growth mindset, learning never ends and your drive to make your program better keeps you improving. I tweak things every season, so the message doesn't get stale. I research successful coaches. I want to tap into their knowledge to make the experience for my players better.

I have a colleague that coaches in a state over eleven-hundred miles away. We both try and do things with our teams that help bring them together. I often run what I call "boot camp" the first week of our season. My colleague has taken the idea and made it even better. My season is in the winter and his is in the spring. We are always asking each other what new idea each of us has tried.

Transformational coaching is sharing. We are not only training our current team for their upcoming season. We are teaching young men and women about life. Our players are eventually entering the workforce. They will become leaders in their professions, leaders of communities, possibly coaches themselves. We may even be coaching the next congressman or president. What lessons have they learned from us? How will they make our world better? That is the real reward, a reward we may never see.

CHAPTER 15
Embracing Diversity

"We need to help students and parents cherish and preserve the ethnic and cultural diversity that nourishes and strengthens this community –and this nation."
–Cesar Chavez

We are experiencing an excellent opportunity for growth in our world at present. People are talking about issues that we have kept buried, just below the surface. Diversity and inclusion are terms that are receiving a lot of attention. Athletics have always provided opportunities to foster diversity. The athletic venue allows players from all different backgrounds and experiences to work together for a common goal.

Anyone who has ever worked with a team or been part of an organization understands that to succeed and reach unknown heights, everyone has to work together. The team needs to work as one. Working as one toward the ultimate prize can only be achieved if a level of trust is developed within the unit.

At one point in my career, I had an assistant coach who did not agree with the direction of our program. This coach had his plan and struggled with the philosophy and direction that I was taking our program. His actions and works necessitated a meeting. We discussed his concerns, and I listened to his interests, I provided an opportunity for him to share his ideas. I shared my plan and my vision once again. When our meeting was over, his words to me were, "I will publicly support you, but privately, I cannot."

What does that mean? It means that we no longer had a trust within our staff. He was telling me that he would act as though we were together, but at home and with his close friends, he would not be supportive. This breakdown of trust harmed our relationship and our team. I did not retain him after the season, and I looked for a coach that would be a better fit for our program.

The same thing happens with players. Our athletes come from many different backgrounds and beliefs. If those beliefs become divisive or create an issue with the team members, then they need to be shared and discussed. Trust among teammates is built on communication and then actions that back up what you say, always remembering that if we can't "walk the talk," then we should not "talk the talk."

This conversation of diversity and inclusion directs us back to the core values we set for our teams. Why is "respect" such a significant core value? It is not only there to teach respect for the game, respect for the officials, and respect for our opponent. It is there so that we respect our teammates and the people that make up our community.

Respect leads to inclusion. Respect leads to discussions about race, sexual orientation, political views, and religions. Our teams can have meaningful conversations about what makes us different, how we see those differences, and how we can support them. I hear many people try to say the "right" thing and profess to be "colorblind." We do not want to go through life being colorblind, but rather we want to be aware of color, race, and the differences between every member of our team as well as what our society can bring to the table.

Communicating and working together help build and strengthen relationships. Healthy relationships bring people. A team that is built on relationships can accomplish goals that were out of reach without it.

As you look at the makeup of your team, your school, and your community, does your coaching staff reflect the composition of your team? Do you have a male staff for a girls' basketball program? Do you have a Caucasian staff for a primarily Latino soccer team?

When I coached a girl's program, I sought out female assistants because players need to see people they can relate to. Girls need to see successful women in their sport. Black and Latino players need to see men and women who look like them and have experienced success in their game and the coaching ranks. Adding diversity to your staff enhances the experiences and a greater understanding for everyone.

As a transformational coach, we realize that our differences make us better. We can challenge each other, and we can enlighten each other. Successful coaches have always been aware of ethnic, religious, and sexual diversity. They have found ways to be inclusive and increase awareness within their teams.

The youth of our country are more color aware. The more we embrace our differences and celebrate them within our circle of influence, the more successful we will be. As coaches, we can be leaders in our communities, and we can have a significant impact on our future leaders. Embracing diversity will lead to greater success.

CHAPTER 16

Practical Applications for Business

"The call it coaching but it's teaching.
You do not just tell them – you show them the reasons."
–Vince Lombardi

My dad was never a coach, but he taught me more about leadership than he could've imagined. My dad was a grocery store manager. He started out as an assistant and was eventually promoted to operating his own store. The small grocery chain he worked for continued to grow and my dad was given larger stores to manage. My dad opened one of the first grocery/department stores in the 70's. Later that decade he opened one of the first warehouse food stores for the company. My dad had a secret and a gift when it came to management. He shared that gift with me.

For my dad, everything he did was about building relationships. He knew his employees, he knew their families, their interests, their highs, and their lows. My dad knew his customers, and he knew his community. People would drive from other cities, pass many other grocery stores to come see my dad and shop at his store. My dad was transformational. My dad connected with people, and he was mindful of everyone around him. My father has since passed, but I try and carry on his legacy of building relationships in every area of my life.

How does a coaching book help a businessman or woman? How does a coaching book help a mother or a father? There have been many different tools that have been provided for you in this book. Communication is a tool that can be very effective and lead to greater success. It is not just about talking, it is about making sure your players, your clients, or your family, understand what you are saying. If your communication uses terminology they do not understand or is not clear to them, it is not their fault when they do not do what was asked. Your message has to be clear, concise, and you must check for understanding.

Leading is about relationships. I believe that I am a successful teacher. I believe this because I listen to my students. I had a principal that recognized that I was successful because of the relationships that I built with my students, their parents, our staff, and the community. My evaluations reflected this, and I was praised because I had a leader that recognized that value.

As I transitioned from a junior high school teacher to a high school teacher, I came under different leadership. When evaluations came out, this new leader valued different measurement criteria. His leadership style was autocratic and things had to be done his way. Every teacher that year was upset with their evaluations. What he valued and what actually worked did not match the things we as teachers were doing. He did not recognize that building relationships led to greater learning and higher performance. My dad, with just a high school diploma, would have done a better job running the school than this principal. As you would probably imagine, that principal did not last long.

You will have greater success as a leader if you take the time to know the stakeholders in your organization. I have already shared the quote, "People do not care what you know, until they know that you care." That is true in the workplace as well as the athletic arena.

I remember that my boys, when they were young, would come home from school, and they would be bouncing off the walls. They ran around the house, they left toys all over the place, they had to be constantly reminded to slow down and put things away. We would go to their parent/teacher conferences and their teachers would praise our boys. They were model students, they were polite, and they helped others. My wife and I would look at each other and shake our heads, 'you're talking about our boys, right?'

Then we learned that we had set an expectation for them in school and in public. We were teaching them to be good and considerate human beings. They worked so hard at school doing the right things that when they got home to a safe environment, they let loose. Their school performance was outstanding because we understood what they needed when they got home.

When you have an employee that changes their behavior at work, and it appears like their performance is slipping, take the time to talk to them. They may have some personal tragedy or conflict they are going through. You may have the power to help that employee and relieve some of the pressure they are under. A good relationship and good communication can help keep the performance level high and still meet the needs of the employee.

We are in a changing world. Our parents would get a job out of high school and stay with that same company until the day they retired. Our players, your employees, will have many different job experiences over their working career. When I left a teaching job to move elsewhere, the superintendent of our school system was not very enthusiastic with the move. The district believed they trained me; they spent a lot of time and money helping me improve. I was theirs, and I should grateful and never leave.

In my new position, the leadership expects their employees to leave. Obviously they would love for all to stay and make a career at that school; however, they recognize that we all have goals, and they encourage our faculty to pursue them. When we have success, it is celebrated. When a colleague moves on to pursue a different passion, they are congratulated, and we follow their new career. It is a different mindset; it is a growth mindset.

We often think we will be happier in our jobs if we were just paid a little more. Then we get paid a little more, and it isn't long before we will be happier if we are paid a little more. The cycle continues until your employer cannot pay you anymore. It doesn't cost a dime to respect your employees. As a leader, you know your hands are tied when pay increases come up, but it costs nothing to be interested in your employees. Compliments and recognition of good work is free.

Compliments may not pay the grocery bill, but feeling valued at work leads to happier employees and happier employees are more productive. As coaches, we pay our athletes with playing time. There are only so many minutes in a contest. The more talented players receive the bulk of the minutes. The more talented employees receive the biggest piece of the financial pie.

Coaches have to keep the players that receive less playing time engaged. Players need recognition when they improve and acknowledgement when they make sacrifices that make the team better.

My dad, while not a coach, lead his store like they were a team long before the business world saw the value in the team. He had his all-star players, the department managers, and the starters, those full-time employees. He also had a bunch of rookies, those part-timers that allowed the starters and all-stars to take a break, a day-off, or a vacation. My dad was able to help each and every employee recognize their role. That recognition led to buy-in, and that buy-in led to my dad having one of the top grossing stores in the company.

If my dad would've been an autocratic leader, turnover would've been high, and the success of the store would have suffered. Transformational leadership works in every environment.

Good luck on your journey!

"Transformational leadership, coaching for mindfulness, pursuing a growth mindset, truly represent a journey of leadership. A journey that you will pursue until you leave this earth. Hopefully I never feel like I've made it, because that means I am done learning."

–Greg Winkler

ABOUT THE AUTHOR

With more than 30 years of experience as an educator, coach and administrator, **Greg Winkler** is currently head coach of the boys' soccer team at Charlotte High School in Punta Gorda, Florida, the same city in which he serves as a physical education teacher at the Charlotte Campus of Florida SouthWestern State College.

A decorated soccer coach in the state of Wisconsin, Winkler was named to the Wisconsin Soccer Association Hall of Fame's Class of 2015 and the Wisconsin Soccer Hall of Fame's Class of 2017, recognizing a coaching career that included more than 400 wins at both the youth and high school levels. In 2018, he was named to the Fond du Lac High School Athletic Hall of Fame, where he enjoyed a 17-year coaching career (1998-2014) that saw him amass the most wins in program history (264).

Among Winkler's many achievements are the National Soccer Coaches Association of America (NSCAA) Coach of the Year Award in 2012 in addition to a trio of United Soccer Coaches, Midwest Regional Coach of the Year Awards (2001, 2004, 2012), and three Fox Valley Association (FVA) Coach of the Year honors. He was also recognized as the Wisconsin Large School Coach of the Year in 2004, the National Federation of State High School Associations (NFHS) Coach of the Year in 2005, and the State Youth Coach of the Year in 2006.

His passion for enhancing the game of soccer in the state extended to all facets of the sport, leading to his involvement as a referee trainer for the Wisconsin Youth Referee Association and a four-year term as president of the Wisconsin Soccer Coaches Association (2002-06), where he was also a director from 2002-2014. Winkler worked with the United Soccer Coaches as the State Technical Director for Wisconsin from 2010-

2013 and has continued his work with the national organization as the high school chair on the advocacy council, a position he's held since 2013.

In 2017, he published a revised edition of his 2009 book, *Coaching a Season of Significance* (Meyer & Meyer Sport), which has been hailed as "a valuable resource for coaches of any sport" and draws upon Winkler's vast experiences to aid coaches in overcoming obstacles on their way to a significant season. Winkler has presented at coaching and athletic director conferences on a variety of topics, ranging from building relationships through athletics to engaging in effective communication with parents and administrators.

A native of Rosendale, Wisconsin, Winkler earned a degree in Secondary Education from the University of Wisconsin-Oshkosh in 1982 and a master's degree in Sports Management from American Public University in 2013. He is a certified athletic administrator and holds a United States Soccer Federation D License as well as United Soccer Coaches, Premier, Advanced National, and National Diplomas. Greg and his wife, Vikki, were recognized as Wisconsin Youth Soccer Association Parents of the Year in 2002.

He and Vikki currently live in Punta Gorda, Florida.

Cover design: Annika Naas
Interior design: Katerina Georgieva
Cover and interior illustration: © Greg Winkler
Layout: Zerosoft
Managing editor: Elizabeth Evans
Copyeditor: Joshua Brazee

THE BEST IN SOCCER!

Paperback, 5.5 x 8.5"
134 pp., b/w
ISBN: 978-1-78255-194-2
$16.95 US

Memmert/Noël

THE PENALTY KICK

THE PSYCHOLOGY OF SUCCESS

This book presents research from over 130 scientific studies on penalty kicks that can be used by athletes, trainers, and managers. All the information on penalty kick methods is based on sport psychology and movement science. The authors have also included anecdotes of the biggest and most important penalties in soccer history. They connect these actual events with the scientific findings, creating real-life examples that make it easier to understand the science. Furthermore, they examine the penalty kick from both the kicker's and goalkeeper's perspectives to explain shooting and saving techniques from every angle.

MEYER & MEYER Sport
Von-Coels-Str. 390
52080 Aachen
Germany

Phone +49 02 41 - 9 58 10 - 13
Fax +49 02 41 - 9 58 10 - 10
E-Mail sales@m-m-sports.com
Website www.m-m-sports.com

MEYER
& MEYER
SPORT

MORE FROM GREG WINKLER!

Paperback, 5.5 x 8.5"
160 pp., b/w
ISBN: 978-1-78255-106-5
$9.95 US

Winkler

COACHING A SEASON OF SIGNIFICANCE

A SOCCER COACHES' COMPANION TO ALL CHALLENGES OF A YEAR

This book was written by an experienced youth and high school soccer coach for other soccer coaches. It takes you from the beginning of the season with the pre-season meeting, organization, and setting goals. It will tackle some of the many challenges and problems coaches must face throughout the course of the season, concluding with the post-season banquet. Coaching a Season of Significance explains how to implement core values for your program, build strong communication, and foster the development of long-lasting relationships.

MEYER & MEYER Sport
Von-Coels-Str. 390
52080 Aachen
Germany

Phone +49 02 41 - 9 58 10 - 13
Fax +49 02 41 - 9 58 10 - 10
E-Mail sales@m-m-sports.com
Website www.m-m-sports.com

MEYER
& MEYER
SPORT